Sunset

Seafood
COOK BOOK

By the Editors of Sunset Books and Sunset Magazine

Lane Publishing Co. ▪ Menlo Park, California

*Sole with Cranberry Butter Sauce
(recipe on page 78) offers bold contrasts
to delight both the eye and the palate.*

Research & Text
Cynthia Scheer

Contributing Editor
Susan Warton

Coordinating Editor
Linda J. Selden

Design
Joe di Chiarro

Illustrations
Susan Jaekel

Photography
Nikolay Zurek

Photo Stylists
Susan Massey-Weil: *2, 7, 10, 15, 18,
23, 26, 31, 34, 39, 42, 47, 50, 55, 58, 71,
74, 79, 82, 87, 95.* **Lynne B. Morrall:**
66. **JoAnn Masaoka Van Atta:** *63, 90.*

Today's Catch

Whether poached, grilled, sauced, or sautéed, served whole, filleted, or in the shell, seafood has nourished us well through the ages. But only recently has it also become highly fashionable—a favorite of celebrated chefs, nutritionists, and people who eat wisely to stay fit.

Along with its companion volume, *Sunset's Fish & Shellfish A to Z*, this cook book belongs in the kitchen of everyone who appreciates the incomparable succulence of seafood. Included among the recipes are many that feature recently introduced seafood discoveries. Only a few years ago, restaurants and markets could offer no more than a handful of choices. But today's fresh catch travels faster and farther to market than ever before, and new technology yields exotic varieties of fish from ocean depths plumbed for the very first time. Let this book guide you to exciting new seafood adventures, as well as to the more familiar, ever-popular standbys.

Our special thanks go to Rebecca LaBrum for her careful editing of the manuscript, to Viki Marugg for her creative contributions to developing the art, and to Sandra Popovich for her design of the photograph on page 87. We also thank Cookin' and Fillamento for their generosity in sharing props for use in our photographs.

For our recipes, we provide a nutritional analysis (please see page 6) prepared by Hill Nutrition Associates, Inc., of New York.

About the Recipes

All of the recipes in this book were tested and developed in the *Sunset* test kitchens.

*Food and Entertaining Editor,
Sunset Magazine*
Jerry Anne Di Vecchio

Cover: A delicate tarragon sauce embellishes salmon, orange roughy, mussels, shrimp, and scallops in Pot-au-Feu de Fruits de Mer (recipe on page 86), a feast of favorite seafood. Design by Susan Bryant. Photography by Nikolay Zurek. Photo styling by Susan Massey-Weil. Food styling by Cynthia Scheer.

Editor, Sunset Books: Elizabeth L. Hogan

First printing September 1989

Contents

Special Features

Seafood

Selecting, Storing & Cooking

There are plenty of fish in the sea, the old saying goes. And today, we're enjoying more of them than ever before. Not long ago, though, the seafood we ate—whether at home or in restaurants—was limited to just a few familiar choices. Salmon, fillet of sole of some kind, and brook trout were typical fish selections; shellfish usually included shrimp, lobster, crab in season (if you were lucky enough to live near the ocean), and possibly scallops.

For many reasons, today's seafood lovers can choose from a much wider array. Restaurants started the trend, preparing an increasing variety of fish and shellfish, often in dazzlingly different ways. Supermarkets followed suit: to serve customers eager to try the new restaurant specialties at home, more stores now feature seafood counters stocked with wares from waters near and far.

Buying Seafood

Freshness is the key to quality in fish and shellfish. From the moment it leaves the water to the time it reaches your market, seafood must be handled properly; if it hasn't been treated well, you'll know by the aroma and appearance.

Your nose is the most reliable judge of freshness. When you sniff seafood, trust your first impression. Truly fresh fish smells like a clean ocean breeze; disagreeable, sweet, or ammonialike odors are caused by bacteria that proliferate as seafood deteriorates.

Fresh fillets and steaks should look moist, lustrous, and cleanly cut, as if just placed on display. The gills of whole fish should be clean and red, not sticky and gray; scales should be shiny and tightly attached to the skin. When you press the flesh, it should feel firm and elastic.

It's more difficult to gauge the freshness of packaged fish, but if you can detect a strong odor straight through the package, don't buy it. Also avoid packages in which liquid has collected, especially if it's cloudy or off-white. If you're purchasing frozen fish, check carefully for signs of mishandling: discoloration, buildup of ice crystals, or drying (especially around the edges).

In choosing fresh hard-shell clams, oysters, and mussels, look for tightly closed shells; if a shell is slightly open, it should close when gently tapped.

Live crabs, lobsters, and crayfish should move their legs. When you pick up a live lobster, its tail will curl beneath its body rather than hang down. Cooked crab or lobster should have a bright red shell and be free of any ammonialike aroma.

Fresh scallops have a slightly sweet smell; their color varies from creamy white to tan or orange and is no indication of quality. If you buy packaged scallops, choose packages containing little or no accumulated liquid.

Fresh shrimp are firm in texture, with a mild, faintly sweet aroma; as they deteriorate, you'll notice an odor of ammonia. Indications of mishandling include black legs, slippery shells, and shells with dark spots or dry-looking patches.

Depending on appetites and the nature of the meal, you'll need $\frac{1}{3}$ to $\frac{1}{2}$ pound of fillets or steaks or $\frac{1}{2}$ to 1 pound whole or cleaned fish per person. Figure on 1 to $1\frac{1}{2}$ pounds mussels or clams in the shell and $\frac{1}{4}$ to $\frac{1}{2}$ pound unshelled shrimp per person.

Storing Seafood

After bringing fish home, unwrap it and rinse it under cool running water; then place it in a container, cover with damp paper towels, and keep in the coldest part of the refrigerator. Cook fresh fish the day you buy it, if possible—within 2 days at the most. Treat shrimp and scallops the same way.

Cover live oysters, clams, mussels, crab, lobster, and crayfish with wet paper towels, then refrigerate; use within 12 hours. It's best to eat fresh-cooked crab or lobster on the day of purchase.

Cooking Guidelines

Though every recipe in this book has its own directions, a few generalizations are in order.

The key to success in cooking fish and shellfish is learning to judge doneness accurately. Seafood cooks so quickly that it's easily overcooked, losing moisture and flavor in the process. Many older recipes recommend cooking fish until the flesh flakes easily when prodded with a fork, but fish that has reached this stage has usually been cooked too long for good flavor and succulence. Another popular method advises cooking fish for 10 minutes for each inch of thickness; but for some preparation techniques, this also may be too long.

We recommend a different test: cut a small slit in the center of thicker fillets, steaks, and whole fish, then check the appearance of the flesh. Fish changes from translucent to opaque as it cooks; when the flesh looks *just slightly translucent or wet inside*, remove the fish from the heat. It will cook a little more from the retained heat. When cooking large fish, you can also insert a meat thermometer in the thickest part, parallel to the backbone; remove the fish from the heat when the thermometer registers 135°F.

The flesh of crab, lobster, scallops, and shrimp turns opaque when cooked. To test, cut to the center of a lobster tail, scallop, or shrimp.

Remove oysters, clams, and mussels from the heat as soon as the shells open. Shucked oysters are cooked when the edges curl.

Cooking Methods

Fish and shellfish are amenable to a variety of cooking methods. As long as you make sure to avoid overcooking (see "Cooking Guidelines," above), you'll get superb results from any of the techniques described here.

Baking. Because fish cooks more slowly in the oven than it does on the grill or rangetop, timing is less critical—there's less chance of overcooking. To keep the fish moist, we suggest preparing it with a sauce, stuffing, or coating.

Fish steaks and fillets at least ¾ inch thick can be baked in sauce. The same treatment works well for whole fish weighing up to 6 pounds. Fish of this size—as well as smaller types such as trout—are also delicious when filled with a rice, mushroom, or bread stuffing before baking.

To bake fish steaks, fillets, and small whole fish more simply, just dip in or brush with melted butter or margarine, then coat with bread crumbs and grated Parmesan cheese or another coating mix.

Barbecuing. The tang of smoke from a barbecue fire is a marvelous accent for full-flavored, at least moderately oily fish such as salmon, swordfish, and tuna. Among shellfish, good choices include skewered scallops and shrimp; you can also set live clams and mussels on the grill just until their shells open. Keep fish and shellfish moist while they cook by brushing with a basting sauce, melted butter or margarine, or oil.

To barbecue by direct heat, set a greased grill 4 to 6 inches above a solid layer of hot or medium coals, as the recipe specifies. Firm-textured fish can go directly on the grill; less sturdy types need the support of a sheet of foil. Cut the foil just large enough to hold the fish without crowding, then grease it and pierce it several times with a skewer to let the smoke through.

Broiling. Like barbecuing, this dry-heat cooking method works best for fish with enough natural oil to stay moist. Choose fish that are at least ½ inch thick; to flavor and moisten them, use a baste or marinade. Kebabs and boned butterflied trout and baby salmon are also good candidates for broiling.

Deep-frying. More than any other cooking method, deep-frying produces a delightful contrast of textures: crisp, golden crust outside, tender seafood inside. Though this technique does add calories, careful attention to temperature minimizes the amount of oil absorbed during cooking. Good choices for deep-frying include fillets or boneless chunks of lean, mild-flavored fish that are moderately firm to firm, such as cod, catfish, rockfish, and snapper; shrimp and squid are excellent, too.

If you don't have a deep-fat fryer, you can deep-fry in a wok or other large pan deep enough to hold 1½ inches of oil when no more than half full. A deep-frying thermometer is an invaluable aid in maintaining the proper cooking temperature.

Pan-frying. You can pan-fry or sauté almost any fish fillet, steak, or small whole fish. For even browning, make sure the seafood is dry and use a pan that heats uniformly. To guarantee a pleasing golden brown exterior, dust the fish lightly with flour or roll in another coating, such as seasoned crumbs, cornmeal, or even sesame seeds.

When pan-frying thin fillets, cook on one side just until the tops look milky white; turn, then begin removing from the pan at once.

Poaching, steaming & steeping. Fish cooks quickly and gently when it's simmered or steeped in liquid or cooked over steam. Suitable for many kinds of fish, these moist-heat methods are also preferred for cooking many shellfish—live crab, lobster, and crayfish; shrimp (see page 51); live clams, oysters, and mussels.

You'll find poaching, steaming, and steeping especially convenient ways to prepare fish for salads or other cold dishes.

Stir-frying. Stir-frying involves rapid stirring and tossing of shellfish or fish cubes or strips over high heat in a wok or large frying pan. When choosing fish to stir-fry, look for nonflaky and firm-textured types that won't break up. Scallops, shrimp, and squid are good shellfish choices.

Serving Seafood Raw

Both *seviche* (raw fish marinated in an acid such as citrus juice) and Japanese *sashimi* (the raw fish served at sushi bars) have become quite popular in recent years. Many diners, though, share a basic concern about these dishes: just how safe to eat is raw fish?

The fact is that many fish do carry parasites, such as roundworm and tapeworm, and some of these can make you sick if ingested in raw fish. They present no danger, however, in adequately cooked or hot-smoked fish; equally safe is fish that has been frozen, either commercially or in a home freezer below 0°F for at least 3 days. (Some authorities advise freezing fish for at least 7 days at -10°F to be absolutely certain of its safety.)

Be careful in choosing fish to eat raw. Tuna is relatively parasite-free, but freshwater fish almost invariably harbor some parasites, as do fish such as salmon that spend part of their life in fresh water. Worms are generally more prevalent in inshore species (such as rockfish and sole) than in deep-sea types like tilefish and mahi mahi.

Though dealers make every effort to remove any worms from fish before it's sold, some do get through. At home, you can hold pieces of fish up to the light to inspect for parasites; most, but not all, are visible. If you find any, cut them out.

If you're ever in doubt about using any fish raw, err on the side of caution: use commercially frozen fish or freeze it at home.

The Best Fish for the Recipe

Most of the recipes in this book offer a choice of fish in the ingredients lists. Let the season, local market availability, family preferences, and your pocketbook guide your selection.

Nutritional Benefits

Seafood supplies high-quality protein for relatively few calories. A 3-ounce serving of lean fish such as cod, sole, halibut, or rockfish usually contains under 100 calories, and even the oilier types (salmon, tuna, mackerel) typically provide no more than 200 calories for a 3-ounce portion.

The fat in all fish and shellfish is mainly polyunsaturated and monounsaturated. Some fish have a unique polyunsaturated fatty acid called omega-3, believed to have a beneficial effect in reducing blood clots, lowering blood cholesterol levels, and preventing heart disease. The fish richest in oil (salmon, tuna, mackerel, sardines, trout, herring, lake whitefish, and sablefish) have the highest omega-3 levels.

Most fish have cholesterol levels about the same as those found in the white meat of poultry or in lean, well-trimmed red meat. Shellfish, once thought to be high-cholesterol as a group, vary in cholesterol content. Shrimp and squid have fairly substantial levels, but other types—clams, mussels, oysters, scallops, crab, and lobster—are actually comparable to most finfish.

In general, fish is low in sodium; shellfish contain more than finfish, but are still considered moderate-sodium foods. If you're on a low-sodium diet, though, do limit your intake of salted or dried fish, pickled herring, smoked fish and shellfish, sardines, and anchovies.

Using Our Nutritional Data

For our recipes, we provide a nutritional analysis stating calorie count; grams of protein, carbohydrates, and total fat; and milligrams of cholesterol and sodium. Generally, the nutritional information applies to a single serving, based on the largest number of servings given for each recipe.

The nutritional analysis does not include optional ingredients or those for which no specific amount is stated. If an ingredient is listed with an option, the information was calculated using the first choice. Likewise, if a range is given for the amount of an ingredient, values were figured based on the first, lower amount.

Many of the recipes in this book give you a choice of fish to use; nutritional content will vary somewhat depending on which type you select.

Dinner from the south of France: Garlic-baked Red Snapper (recipe on page 83), cooked to moist perfection with herbs, new potatoes, and halved heads of aromatic garlic. Serve with a lettuce and tomato salad, a warm baguette, and a chilled blush wine.

A Buying Guide to Common Fish

Name & Related Species	Taste & Texture	Size & Forms	Cooking Methods
Bass (striped bass, white bass)	Mild, slightly sweet; flaky, lean	½ to 10 lbs.; whole	Bake, barbecue, pan-fry, poach, steam
Bluefish	Rich, distinctive; soft, moist, moderately oily	3 to 6 lbs.; whole, fillets	Bake, barbecue, broil, pan-fry, smoke
Buffalo	Mild, slightly earthy; moist, tender, oily	2 to 12 lbs.; whole, steaks	Bake, barbecue, broil, poach, steam, smoke
Catfish	Mild, sweet, slightly earthy; moist, flaky, moderately lean	1½ to 5 lbs.; whole, fillets, steaks	Bake, barbecue, broil, deep-fry, pan-fry, poach, steam
Cod (Atlantic cod, Pacific cod, haddock, pollock, Antarctic whiting or queen, hoki)	Mild; tender, medium-firm to soft flakes, lean	Under 10 lbs.; fillets	Bake, barbecue, deep-fry, pan-fry, poach
Croaker (Atlantic croaker, spot)	Mild; moist, flaky, moderately lean	Under 1 to 1½ lbs.; whole	Bake, barbecue, broil, pan-fry, poach, steam
Drum (red drum or redfish, black drum)	Mild to moderately pronounced; tender-firm, moist, lean	Under 10 lbs. best; fillets	Bake, barbecue, pan-fry, poach, steam
Flounder/Sole (gray sole, winter flounder, American plaice, yellowtail flounder, summer flounder or fluke, petrale sole, sand sole, English sole, rex sole, Pacific sanddab, Dover sole, California halibut)	Mild, sometimes sweet, nutlike; tender-firm to soft, lean	Under ½ to 20 lbs. Whole, fillets; large species may be cut into steaks	Bake (thick fillets or steaks), deep-fry (strips from thick fillets), pan-fry, poach (thick fillets or rolled-up thin fillets)
Halibut (Pacific halibut, Atlantic halibut)	Mild, sweet; fine-grained with dense, firm flakes, lean	Up to 300 lbs.; steaks, fillets, roasts	Bake, barbecue (skewer for kebabs), pan-fry, stir-fry, poach, steam
Herring/Sardine (Atlantic herring, Pacific herring, Pacific sardine)	Pronounced flavor; soft, tender, oily	1 lb. or less; whole	Bake, barbecue, broil, pan-fry
Jack (amberjack, yellowtail, jack cravalle)	Rich but mild; firm to meaty, moderately oily	2 to over 100 lbs.; steaks, fillets	Bake, barbecue, or broil (skewer for kebabs), pan-fry, stir-fry, poach, smoke
Lingcod	Mild; tender-firm, moist flakes, very lean	About 10 lbs.; fillets, steaks	Bake, barbecue, deep-fry, pan-fry
Mackerel (Atlantic, Spanish, king, cero, Pacific, and Pacific jack mackerel; wahoo or ono)	Mild to strong; moist, tender (king and wahoo firm), lean to oily	Under 1 to 35 lbs.; whole, fillets, steaks	Bake, barbecue, broil, pan-fry, poach (mild species), smoke
Mahi Mahi	Sweet, distinctive; tender-firm, lean	10 to 40 lbs.; fillets, steaks	Bake, barbecue, pan-fry, poach, steam
Monkfish	Sweet, lobsterlike; chewy, nonflaky, lean	Up to 50 lbs.; tapering tail fillets	Bake, barbecue, or broil as cubes, deep-fry, pan-fry, stir-fry, poach
Mullet (striped mullet)	Rich, moderately pronounced; medium-firm, tender	Under 2 lbs.; whole	Bake, barbecue, poach, steam, smoke

Name & Related Species	Taste & Texture	Size & Forms	Cooking Methods
Orange Roughy	Mild, sweet; moist, tender-firm	About 3 lbs.; fillets	Bake, barbecue, broil, deep-fry, pan-fry, poach, steam
Perch (walleye, yellow perch)	Mild, delicate, sweet; tender-firm, lean	¼ to 3 lbs.; whole, fillets	Bake, deep-fry, pan-fry, poach, steam
Pompano (Florida pompano)	Sweet, rich; tender-firm, moist	About 2 lbs.; whole	Bake, barbecue, pan-fry, poach, steam
Rockfish (Atlantic and Pacific ocean perch, Pacific rockfish, often called Pacific snapper)	Mild; tender-firm, moist, flaky, lean	2 to 5 lbs.; whole, fillets	Bake, barbecue, deep-fry, pan-fry, poach
Sablefish (sometimes called black cod or butterfish)	Rich, mild; velvety soft, tender, oily	3 to 10 lbs.; fillets	Bake, barbecue, broil, pan-fry, steam, smoke
Salmon (Atlantic, king or chinook, silver or coho, pink, sockeye, chum salmon)	Delicate to rich; moist, flaky, tender, medium to high fat	1 to 100 lbs.; whole, steaks, fillets, roasts	Bake, barbecue, broil, pan-fry, poach, steam
Sea Bass/Grouper (black and white sea bass, black and red grouper, Chilean sea bass)	Mild; firm to meaty, lean (Chilean sea bass is richer, softer)	1 to over 50 lbs.; whole, fillets	Bake, barbecue, pan-fry, stir-fry, poach, steam
Seatrout/Weakfish (spotted seatrout, gray weakfish)	Mild, sweet; fine-grained, moist	½ to 3 lbs.; whole, fillets	Bake, barbecue, pan-fry, poach, steam
Shad & Roe	Rich, sweet; soft, oily	3 to 5 lbs.; whole, fillets, roe only	Barbecue, broil; pan-fry fillets and roe
Shark (thresher, soupfin, bonito, blacktip, mako, sandbar shark)	Mild to moderately pronounced; firm, dense, meaty, lean	35 to over 1000 lbs.; steaks, fillets	Bake, barbecue (skewer for kebabs), pan-fry, stir-fry, poach
Smelt (rainbow and eulachon or Columbia River smelt, grunion, silversides)	Delicate; tender, soft to firmer	3 to 8 inches long; whole	Bake, barbecue, broil, deep-fry, pan-fry
Snapper (red snapper and other Florida and Caribbean snappers)	Mild, distinctive; tender-firm, lean	4 to 6 lbs.; whole, fillets	Bake, barbecue, pan-fry, poach, steam
Sturgeon	Mild but distinctive; firm, meaty, moderately oily	10 to 80 lbs.; chunks, steaks, fillets	Bake, barbecue, or broil (skewer for kebabs), pan-fry, poach, smoke
Swordfish	Mild but distinctively rich; firm, meaty, moderately oily	50 to 200 lbs.; boneless chunks, steaks	Bake, barbecue, or broil (skewer for kebabs), pan-fry, stir-fry, poach
Tilapia	Mild, sweet, slightly earthy; moist, tender, lean	1 to 1½ lbs.; whole, fillets	Bake, barbecue, deep-fry, pan-fry, poach, steam
Trout (rainbow trout, steelhead trout)	Mild; tender, flaky, moderately lean	½ to 2 lbs.; whole, boned and butterflied	Bake, barbecue, broil, pan-fry, poach, steam, smoke
Tuna (albacore, bluefin, yellowfin, bigeye)	Rich, distinctive; meaty, firm, lean to oily	10 to 1000 lbs.; boneless loins, steaks, fillets	Bake, barbecue, broil, pan-fry, poach, steam, smoke
Whitefish (lake whitefish)	Rich, mild; tender, flaky, oily	1 to 4 lbs.; whole, fillets	Bake, barbecue, broil, pan-fry, poach, smoke

Seafood appetizers are party fare. At left, Smoked
Salmon Mayonnaise (recipe on page 17) tops cucumber
rounds. Hot tidbits include Cheddar Cheese Puffs with
Smoked Trout Mousse (recipe on page 17), Shrimp & Feta
Fila Triangles (recipe on page 16), and Smoked Salmon &
Herbed Cheese Tarts (recipe on page 16).

Appetizers

Fish and shellfish show up as appetizer favorites at all the best parties. Glistening fresh oysters on the half shell and succulent shrimp with cocktail sauce are classics—but the new and varied seafood choices on the market today inspire an expanded hors d'oeuvre and first-course repertoire. Try a tangy seviche of fresh tuna or scallops, romaine-wrapped grilled fish, or tender squid with shiitake mushrooms. You'll also find that shellfish and smoked fish bring distinction to any assortment of bite-size morsels, hot or cold, to serve with apéritifs or sparkling wine.

Tahitian-style Tuna Seviche

Preparation time: About 35 minutes

Chilling time: About 1 hour

Evocative of the tropics, this tangy interpretation of seviche features fresh tuna, ginger, and coconut milk—ingredients once considered exotic, but now widely available in much of the country.

- 1 **pound boneless and skinless fresh tuna, such as albacore, bluefin, or yellowfin (see page 6 for tips on using raw fish)**
- ¾ **cup lime or lemon juice**
- ½ **cup canned or thawed frozen unsweetened coconut milk**
- ¼ **teaspoon coconut extract**
- 2 **tablespoons sugar**
- 1 **tablespoon minced fresh ginger**
- ½ **medium-size red bell pepper, seeded and finely chopped**
- ½ **cup thinly sliced green onions (including tops)**
  Salt
  Butter lettuce leaves, washed and crisped
- 1 **medium-size carrot, finely shredded**
- ½ **medium-size cucumber, peeled and thinly sliced**
- 1 **medium-size tomato, cut into thin wedges**

Rinse tuna and pat dry; chop very finely. Place in a bowl; stir in lime juice. Cover and refrigerate until surface of fish is light in color (about 1 hour). Drain fish in a fine wire strainer, discarding lime juice; then return fish to bowl and add coconut milk, coconut extract, sugar, ginger, bell pepper, and onions. Mix well; season to taste with salt. Spoon into a serving bowl.

On a platter, arrange lettuce, carrot, cucumber, and tomato. To serve, spoon small portions of vegetables onto lettuce; top with tuna mixture. Eat with knife and fork, or roll up and eat out of hand. Makes 12 first-course servings.

Per serving: 92 calories, 9 g protein, 5 g carbohydrates, 4 g total fat, 14 mg cholesterol, 22 mg sodium

Pickled Salmon

Preparation time: About 15 minutes

Standing time: 30 minutes

Cooking time: 30 minutes

Chilling time: At least 24 hours

Entice guests with chunks of spicy pickled salmon, served with crunchy rye crackers or nestled in crisp leaves of butter lettuce.

- 2½ **pounds skinless salmon fillets**
- 1 **tablespoon salt**
- 2 **cups** *each* **distilled white vinegar and water**
- ¼ **cup salad oil**
- 1½ **tablespoons mixed pickling spices**
- 1 **teaspoon salt**
- 5 **small white boiling onions, thinly sliced**

Rinse salmon, pat dry, and cut into ¾-inch chunks; remove any small bones. Spread fish in a single layer on a piece of wax paper or in a shallow glass baking dish. Sprinkle with the 1 tablespoon salt and let stand, uncovered, for 30 minutes. Rinse fish well and pat dry.

While salmon is standing, combine vinegar, water, oil, pickling spices, and the 1 teaspoon salt in a 2- to 3-quart pan. Bring to a boil over high heat; then reduce heat, partially cover, and simmer for 30 minutes.

Layer fish chunks and onions in a 2- to 2½-quart wide-mouth jar or bowl. Pour the simmering pickling liquid over fish and onions, cover loosely, and let cool. Then cover tightly and refrigerate for at least 24 hours or up to a week.

Transfer fish and onions with some of the pickling liquid to a serving bowl and provide picks for spearing; or spoon fish and onions onto individual plates and eat with forks. Makes about 6 cups.

Per ¼ cup: 80 calories, 9 g protein, .66 g carbohydrates, 4 g total fat, 26 mg cholesterol, 158 mg sodium

Lox Roses with Cilantro Sauce

Preparation time: About 20 minutes

Fanciful smoked-salmon roses "floating" in piquant cilantro sauce make a colorful first course for a warm-weather dinner.

- ½ **pound thinly sliced lox**
- 2 **medium-size tomatoes, peeled and seeded**
- 1½ **cups firmly packed fresh cilantro (coriander) sprigs**
- 2 **tablespoons** *each* **lemon juice and salad oil**
- 1 **tablespoon drained green peppercorns**
  Fresh cilantro (coriander) sprigs

Divide lox into 4 equal portions. Loosely roll each portion into a spiral to form a rose. (Or roll each portion into several smaller spirals, forming smaller roses.) Set aside.

In a blender or food processor, whirl tomatoes, the 1½ cups cilantro sprigs, lemon juice, oil, and peppercorns until smoothly puréed; pour a fourth of the sauce onto each of 4 salad plates.

Set lox roses in sauce, flattening bases slightly so roses will stand up. Garnish with cilantro sprigs and serve at once (sauce separates as it stands). Makes 4 first-course servings.

Per serving: 141 calories, 11 g protein, 3 g carbohydrates, 9 g total fat, 13 mg cholesterol, 1,198 mg sodium

Salmon or Cod Jerky

Preparation time: 20 minutes

Standing time: 5 to 15 minutes

Drying time: 5 to 6 hours

Seasoned and dried like its meaty counterpart, fish jerky is a savory snack or appetizer. It's a natural for trail or campsite munching, too, since it needn't be refrigerated. If you like chewy jerky, slice the fish with the grain; for a more tender texture, cut across the grain.

- 2 **pounds skinless salmon or cod fillets, partially frozen**
- ½ **cup soy sauce**
- 2 **tablespoons sugar**
- ½ **teaspoon minced fresh ginger**
  Freshly ground pepper

Rinse salmon and pat dry. Slice with or across the grain into ¼-inch-thick strips; remove any small bones.

In a wide frying pan, combine soy sauce, sugar, and ginger. Bring to a boil over high heat; remove from heat. Add fish strips and mix lightly to coat; then let stand for 5 minutes for lightly seasoned jerky, 15 minutes for more flavorful jerky. Lift strips from marinade. Arrange close together (but not overlapping) on wire racks set in rimmed shallow baking pans (lined with foil, if desired); or arrange on dehydrator racks. Sprinkle strips with pepper, then turn strips over and sprinkle with pepper on other side.

Dry fish in a 150° oven or dehydrator until strips feel leathery, firm, and dry (5 to 6 hours). If you're using an oven, switch positions of pans every hour to ensure even drying. Let jerky cool completely, then remove from racks and store in airtight containers. Jerky keeps almost indefinitely. Makes about ¾ pound.

Per ounce: 111 calories, 15 g protein, .76 g carbohydrates, 5 g total fat, 42 mg cholesterol, 205 mg sodium

Scallop Terrine with Capers

Preparation time: About 15 minutes

Baking time: 40 to 50 minutes

Chilling time: At least 6 hours

Scallops and white fish are perfect partners in this cool, caper-accented first course. Because the terrine must chill for at least 6 hours, you'll need to prepare it well ahead of time.

- **14** green onions
- **½** pound skinless white-fleshed fish fillets, such as cod, rockfish, or orange roughy
- **½** pound scallops, rinsed and drained
- **1** egg
- **⅓** cup whipping cream
- **½** teaspoon dry tarragon
- **¼** teaspoon ground white pepper
- **2** tablespoons drained capers
  About ½ teaspoon salt
  Green Onion Mayonnaise (recipe follows)
  Lemon wedges
  Butter lettuce leaves, washed and crisped (optional)

Trim and discard roots from onions. Thinly slice white parts of 6 of the onions; set aside. Cover and refrigerate green tops to use in Green Onion Mayonnaise.

Rinse fish, pat dry, and cut into ½-inch-square chunks; remove any small bones. In a food processor, combine fish, sliced onions, scallops, egg, cream, tarragon, and pepper; whirl until smoothly puréed. (Or, using a food chopper fitted with the fine blade, grind sliced onions, fish, and scallops into a bowl. Add egg, cream, tarragon, and pepper; mix well.) Stir in capers; season to taste with salt.

Spread the fish purée in a greased 4½- by 8½-inch loaf pan. Cover and place in a larger baking pan. Pour boiling water into larger pan to about half the depth of loaf pan.

Bake in a 350° oven until terrine feels set when lightly touched in center (40 to 50 minutes). Lift terrine from water, uncover, and let cool. Cover and refrigerate until cold and firm (at least 6 hours) or until next day. Prepare Green Onion Mayonnaise.

Slice terrine ½ inch thick, lift slices from pan, and place 2 slices on each of 8 salad plates. Garnish plates with remaining 8 whole green onions, lemon wedges, and lettuce (if desired). Spoon a dollop of Green Onion Mayonnaise onto each plate. Makes 8 first-course servings.

Green Onion Mayonnaise. Thinly slice the 6 **reserved green onion tops** and whirl in a blender with ½ cup **mayonnaise** and 1 tablespoon **lemon juice** until smoothly puréed. Stir in 1 tablespoon drained **capers.** If made ahead, cover and refrigerate for up to a day.

Per serving: 196 calories, 12 g protein, 3 g carbohydrates, 15 g total fat, 73 mg cholesterol, 373 mg sodium

---

To Prepare Mussels

Inspect mussels carefully to make sure they're alive; the shells should be tightly closed or, if open, should close when lightly tapped. Clean mussels just before cooking, since they don't live long afterwards.

To clean, first scrape off any barnacles (they're inclined to hold sand). Pull off the tough brown hairlike "beard" with a quick tug; then scrub mussels with a stiff brush under cold running water and rinse well.

Honeydew & Scallop Seviche

Preparation time: About 15 minutes

Chilling time: At least 8 hours

Tender scallops join sweet honeydew melon to make this cool and refreshing first course. Assemble the seviche and slice the melon in the morning or even a day in advance; at serving time, you need only assemble the plates.

- ½ **pound bay scallops or sea scallops**
- 1 **honeydew melon (2 to 3 lbs.)**
- ⅓ **cup lemon juice**
- ¼ **cup finely chopped onion**
- 1 **or 2 fresh jalapeño or serrano chiles, seeded and finely chopped**
- 2 **tablespoons olive oil or salad oil**
- ½ **teaspoon chopped fresh oregano leaves or ⅛ teaspoon dry oregano leaves**
  About ½ teaspoon salt
- ¼ **cup finely chopped green bell pepper**
- 2 **teaspoons minced fresh cilantro (coriander)**
- 4 **fresh cilantro (coriander) sprigs**
- 4 **lemon wedges**

If using sea scallops, cut them into ½-inch pieces. Rinse and drain scallops; set aside.

Cut melon lengthwise into quarters; scoop out and discard seeds. Using a grapefruit knife, cut off and discard rind. Cut 3 of the melon quarters crosswise into ¼-inch slices and set aside; dice remaining melon.

In a large bowl, stir together scallops, diced melon, lemon juice, onion, chiles, oil, and oregano; season to taste with salt. Cover scallop mixture and melon slices separately; refrigerate, stirring scallop mixture occasionally, for at least 8 hours or up to a day. When scallops are ready to serve, they should be opaque throughout; cut to test.

To serve, stir bell pepper and minced cilantro into scallop mixture. Fan melon slices out on 4 salad plates. Spoon a fourth of the scallop mixture at the base of each melon fan. Garnish each serving with a cilantro sprig and a lemon wedge. Makes 4 first-course servings.

Per serving: 157 calories, 10 g protein, 14 g carbohydrates, 7 g total fat, 19 mg cholesterol, 380 mg sodium

Pictured on facing page

Mussels on Lemon-Garlic Toast

Preparation time: About 15 minutes

Cooking time: 12 to 15 minutes

Chilling time: At least 30 minutes

Start off a memorable feast with mussels steamed in white wine, presented on the half shell with toasted French bread. Each crisp baguette slice gets a tantalizing topping: a drizzling of the concentrated cooking juices, accented with lemon and garlic.

- 12 **mussels in shells**
- 1 **cup dry white wine**
- ¾ **teaspoon finely shredded lemon peel**
- 1 **clove garlic, minced or pressed**
- 1 **tablespoon *each* finely chopped parsley and extra-virgin olive oil**
  Salt and pepper
  Baguette Toast (recipe follows)
  Lemon slices
  Italian parsley sprigs

Prepare mussels (see page 13). Place mussels in a wide frying pan, add wine, cover, and bring to a boil over high heat. Reduce heat to low and simmer until mussels open (about 5 minutes). Lift mussels from pan with a slotted spoon and transfer to a bowl; reserve cooking liquid in pan. Discard any unopened mussels; cover remaining mussels and refrigerate until cool (at least 30 minutes).

Meanwhile, boil cooking liquid over high heat, uncovered, until reduced to about 3 tablespoons (4 to 5 minutes); remove from heat. Stir in lemon peel, garlic, chopped parsley, and oil; season to taste with salt and pepper. Cover and refrigerate until cool (at least 15 minutes). Prepare Baguette Toast.

To serve, remove and discard top shells from mussels. Place 3 mussels on half shells on each of 4 salad plates; arrange 3 toast slices on each plate. Drizzle lemon-garlic mixture over toast. Garnish with lemon slices and parsley sprigs. To eat, pluck mussels from shells with a small fork and place on toast. Makes 4 first-course servings.

Baguette Toast. Cut 1 **French bread baguette** (8 oz.) into ½-inch-thick diagonal slices. Lay slices in a single layer on a large baking sheet. Broil about 4 inches below heat until golden on both sides, turning once (about 2 minutes *total*).

Per serving: 219 calories, 8 g protein, 33 g carbohydrates, 6 g total fat, 8 mg cholesterol, 401 mg sodium

Splendor on the half shell: Mussels on Lemon-Garlic Toast (recipe on facing page). The succulent steamed shellfish and crisp baguette slices make an exquisitely elegant first course.

Seafood Party Fare

Succulent, versatile fish and shellfish are consummate party foods. Irresistible when baked in delicate fila dough or tender-crisp puff pastry, seafood also makes a tempting filling for cheese-dappled tart or cream puff shells. And few guests will be able to forgo the rich pleasure of sweet, creamy crab in a cool endive spear or smoked salmon mayonnaise spread on a crisp cucumber slice.

Shrimp & Feta Fila Triangles

Pictured on page 10

Shrimp & Feta Cheese Filling (recipe follows)
6 **sheets fila pastry (about ¼ of a 1-lb. package), thawed if frozen**
About ½ cup (¼ lb.) **butter or margarine, melted**

Prepare Shrimp & Feta Cheese Filling and set aside. Unroll fila and lay flat; cut sheets in half crosswise and cover with plastic wrap to prevent drying.

Brush a half-sheet of fila with butter, keeping remainder of fila covered. Cut buttered fila half-sheet lengthwise into thirds. Place about 1½ teaspoons of the filling in upper corner of each strip and fold corner down over filling to make a triangle. Fold triangle over onto itself. Then continue folding triangle from side to side all down length of strip, as if you were folding a flag. Place triangles about 1½ inches apart on greased baking sheets. Brush tops with butter and cover with plastic wrap while shaping remaining pastries.

(At this point, you may freeze pastries for up to 1 month. To freeze, place shaped pastries in freezer until firm; then carefully stack in a rigid container, placing foil between each layer. Do not thaw before baking.)

Bake pastries in a 375° oven until well browned and crisp (10 to 15 minutes; about 35 minutes if frozen). Serve hot or at room temperature. Makes 3 dozen appetizers.

Shrimp & Feta Cheese Filling. Crumble 6 ounces **feta cheese** into a bowl. Mix in ½ pound **tiny cooked and shelled shrimp,** ⅛ teaspoon *each* **ground white pepper** and **dill weed,** and ¼ cup chopped **parsley.**

Per appetizer: 51 calories, 2 g protein, 2 g carbohydrates, 4 g total fat, 23 mg cholesterol, 93 mg sodium

Smoked Salmon & Herbed Cheese Tarts

Pictured on page 10

1 **sheet (half of a 17¼-oz. package) frozen puff pastry**
⅓ **cup (about 2 oz.) shredded or finely chopped smoked salmon**
4 **ounces cream cheese flavored with herbs and garlic, at room temperature**
Small fresh marjoram or parsley sprigs (optional)

Thaw pastry at room temperature for 20 minutes, then unfold on a lightly floured board and roll out to make an 11-inch square. Cut pastry into 2-inch circles; reroll scraps and cut again. Fit circles lightly into bottoms and partway up sides of 1¾-inch muffin cups.

In a small bowl, mix salmon into cream cheese. Fill each pastry shell with a scant teaspoon of cheese mixture. Cover and refrigerate for at least 30 minutes or up to 2 hours. Bake tarts in a 450° oven until golden brown (12 to 15 minutes). Garnish with marjoram sprigs, if desired. Makes about 3 dozen appetizers.

Per appetizer: 41 calories, .83 g protein, 3 g carbohydrates, 3 g total fat, 4 mg cholesterol, 58 mg sodium

Bay Scallop Tarts

Cheese Tart Shells (recipe follows)
⅓ **cup *each* dry white wine and whipping cream**
2 **teaspoons lemon juice**
1 **teaspoon Dijon mustard**
¼ **teaspoon dry tarragon**
1 **small shallot, finely chopped**
½ **pound bay scallops, rinsed and drained**
2 **tablespoons grated Parmesan cheese**

Prepare Cheese Tart Shells; let cool, then remove from pans. Set aside.

In a wide frying pan, combine wine, cream, lemon juice, mustard, tarragon, and shallot. Bring to a boil over medium-high heat. Add scallops and cook, uncovered, stirring often, just until scallops are opaque throughout; cut to test (2 to 3 minutes). Remove from heat. Lift scallops from pan with a slotted spoon, drain, and spoon evenly into tart shells.

Return pan with liquid to high heat. Bring to a boil; boil, uncovered, until large, shiny bubbles form and liquid is reduced by about half. Spoon reduced liquid over scallops. Top with cheese. (At this point, you may cover lightly and refrigerate for up to 4 hours.)

Arrange tarts on a baking sheet. Bake in a 400° oven until heated through (5 to 10 minutes). Makes 15 appetizers.

Cheese Tart Shells. In a large bowl, combine ¾ cup **all-purpose flour,** ⅓ cup finely shredded **Swiss cheese,** and 2 tablespoons grated **Parmesan**

cheese. Cut in ¼ cup cold **butter** or margarine until mixture resembles coarse crumbs. Drizzle with ½ teaspoon **Worcestershire**. Gradually mix in 1½ to 3 tablespoons **cold water** until dough begins to cling together; with your hands, press dough into a firm ball.

Divide dough into 15 equal portions. Press each portion into a shallow 1½- to 2-inch tart pan to make a ½- to ¾-inch-deep shell. Pierce each shell in several places with a fork. Arrange tart pans on a large baking sheet. Bake in a 400° oven until pastry is golden brown (12 to 15 minutes). Transfer pans to racks; let tart shells cool, then carefully remove from pans.

Per appetizer: 95 calories, 5 g protein, 6 g carbohydrates, 6 g total fat, 22 mg cholesterol, 101 mg sodium

Cheddar Cheese Puffs with Smoked Trout Mousse

Pictured on page 10

1 cup water
½ cup (¼ lb.) butter or margarine
⅛ teaspoon ground nutmeg
1 cup all-purpose flour
4 eggs
½ cup finely shredded, lightly packed sharp Cheddar cheese
    Smoked Trout Mousse (recipe follows)

In a 2- to 3-quart pan, bring water, butter, and nutmeg to a full boil over medium-high heat, stirring until butter is melted. Add flour all at once and stir briskly until mixture leaves sides of pan and forms a ball (about 2 minutes). Remove from heat and transfer to a bowl; let stand for about 5 minutes.

Add eggs, one at a time, beating after each addition until mixture is well blended. Stir in cheese. Scoop out spoonfuls of dough about 1½ inches in diameter; drop at least 1 inch apart onto greased large baking sheets.

Bake in a 400° oven until puffs are golden brown (20 to 25 minutes). Turn off oven. Remove puffs from oven and pierce each in several places with a fork. Return to baking sheets in turned-off oven for 10 minutes to crisp. Let cool on racks while preparing Smoked Trout Mousse.

Cut each cheese puff in half crosswise. Spoon mousse equally into bottom half of each puff; replace tops. Refrigerate until serving time; serve within 2 hours. Makes about 3 dozen appetizers.

Smoked Trout Mousse. In a large bowl, combine 1 cup **whipping cream**, 1½ tablespoons **lemon juice**, and ⅛ teaspoon *each* **salt** and **ground white pepper.** Beat until stiff. Fold in 1 tablespoon **prepared horseradish** and ⅔ cup finely chopped boneless and skinless **smoked trout.**

Per appetizer: 74 calories, 2 g protein, 3 g carbohydrates, 6 g total fat, 49 mg cholesterol, 78 mg sodium

Smoked Salmon Mayonnaise on Cucumber Rounds

Pictured on page 10

3 ounces smoked salmon or lox, coarsely chopped (about ½ cup)
1 egg yolk
1½ tablespoons lemon juice
3 tablespoons salad oil (see Note)
1 European or English cucumber (about 1 lb.), cut into ⅛-inch-thick slices
    Finely chopped mild red onion
    Watercress sprigs
    Thin lemon wedges

In a blender or food processor, combine salmon, egg yolk, and lemon juice; whirl until puréed. With motor running, add oil in a thin, steady stream, mixing until smoothly blended. Cover and refrigerate until cold and thick (at least 1 hour or until next day).

Pipe or spoon about 1 teaspoon of the salmon mixture onto each cucumber slice. Arrange on a serving plate and garnish with onion, watercress sprigs, and lemon wedges. Makes about 64 appetizers.

Note: If you use dry, Indian-type smoked salmon rather than moist, lox-style salmon, increase amount of oil to ¼ cup.

Per appetizer: 9 calories, .31 g protein, .22 g carbohydrates, .76 g total fat, 5 mg cholesterol, 11 mg sodium

Creamy Crab in Endive Spears

1 small package (3 oz.) cream cheese, at room temperature
2 tablespoons sour cream
2 teaspoons lime or lemon juice
¼ teaspoon grated lime or lemon peel
2 tablespoons chopped chives
¼ pound cooked crabmeat
    Salt and ground white pepper
4 to 6 heads Belgian endive, separated into leaves, washed, and crisped

In small bowl of an electric mixer, beat cream cheese, sour cream, and lime juice until well blended and fluffy. Mix in lime peel, chives, and crab; season to taste with salt and pepper.

Pipe or spoon a dollop of crab mixture into wide part of each endive spear. Arrange spears on a serving plate in a starburst pattern, tips pointing outward. If made ahead, cover lightly and refrigerate for up to 4 hours. Makes about 3½ dozen appetizers.

Per appetizer: 12 calories, .76 g protein, .24 g carbohydrates, .88 g total fat, 5 mg cholesterol, 14 mg sodium

Dainty offerings on the hors d'oeuvre tray, Sautéed Squid
& Shiitake Mushrooms on Rye Rounds (recipe on page
20) sparkle with sweet-tart raspberry vinegar. A garnish
of juicy fresh berries brings out the fruit flavor.

Bell Pepper & Smoked Oyster Boats

Preparation time: About 35 minutes

Load each red bell pepper raft with a tempting cargo of seasoned cream cheese, smoked oysters, and chives.

    4 medium-size red bell peppers
    1 can (3¾ oz.) small smoked oysters, drained
    2 small packages (3 oz. *each*) cream cheese, at room temperature
    2 tablespoons lemon juice
    1 teaspoon celery seeds
   64 chive pieces (*each* 4 inches long)

Cut each bell pepper lengthwise into 8 equal wedges; cut out and discard seeds. If necessary, cut larger oysters in half so you have a total of 32 pieces.

In a small bowl, beat cream cheese, lemon juice, and celery seeds until smooth. Spread about 1 teaspoon of the mixture over 1½ inches at end of each pepper strip; top with an oyster and 2 chive pieces. If made ahead, cover and refrigerate for up to a day. Makes 32 appetizers.

Per appetizer: 25 calories, .86 g protein, .92 g carbohydrates, 2 g total fat, 9 mg cholesterol, 37 mg sodium

Creamy Crab Dip

Preparation time: About 15 minutes

Spoon this luscious crabmeat dip into the centers of cold cooked artichokes for an impressive first course. Or surround it with crisp raw vegetables such as baby carrots, cucumber slices, cauliflowerets, and blanched and chilled Chinese pea pods.

    1 large package (8 oz.) cream cheese, at room temperature
    2 tablespoons *each* dry white wine and lemon juice
    ¼ cup thinly sliced green onions (including tops)
    1 clove garlic, minced or pressed
    1 teaspoon Dijon mustard
    ½ teaspoon Worcestershire
    ½ pound cooked crabmeat
       Salt and pepper
       Cold cooked artichokes or raw vegetables of your choice

In large bowl of an electric mixer, beat cream cheese until smooth. Gradually beat in wine and lemon

juice until blended. Mix in onions, garlic, mustard, and Worcestershire. Stir in crab until well blended. Season to taste with salt and pepper. If made ahead, cover and refrigerate for up to a day.

Serve as a dip for artichokes or raw vegetables. Makes about 2 cups (8 servings).

Per tablespoon: 33 calories, 2 g protein, .34 g carbohydrates, 3 g total fat, 15 mg cholesterol, 47 mg sodium

Potted Shrimp with Chervil

Preparation time: About 25 minutes

Cooking time: 6 to 8 minutes

Chilling time: At least 2 hours

Standing time: About 30 minutes

Gently cooked, then puréed with butter and herbs, fresh shrimp make a delicate spread for baguette toast or buttery crackers. Steep the shrimp as the recipe directs, or cook them in your microwave oven (see page 20).

    1   quart water
    1   pound medium-size raw shrimp (30 to 50 per lb.)
    ½   cup (¼ lb.) butter or margarine, at room temperature
    1½ tablespoons lime or lemon juice
    ¼   teaspoon salt
    ⅛   teaspoon ground white pepper
    ¼   cup lightly packed fresh chervil
        Fresh chervil sprigs
        Toasted French bread baguette slices

In a 3- to 4-quart pan, bring water to a boil over high heat. Remove pan from heat and quickly add unshelled shrimp. Cover tightly and let stand until shrimp are opaque throughout; cut to test (6 to 8 minutes). Drain; cool quickly in cold water and drain again. Shell and devein.

In a food processor, combine shrimp, butter, lime juice, salt, and pepper. Whirl until shrimp are finely chopped and mixture is well combined. Add the ¼ cup chervil and whirl again until blended. Spoon mixture into a 2½-cup ramekin or bowl. To blend flavors, cover and refrigerate for at least 2 hours or up to a day. To serve, let stand at room temperature for about 30 minutes, then garnish with chervil sprigs and serve with toasted baguette slices. Makes about 2 cups.

Per tablespoon: 38 calories, 2 g protein, .16 g carbohydrates, 3 g total fat, 25 mg cholesterol, 63 mg sodium

Pictured on page 18

Sautéed Squid & Shiitake Mushrooms on Rye Rounds

Preparation time: About 15 minutes

Soaking time (if using dried mushrooms): About 30 minutes

Cooking time: About 15 minutes

A tingle of raspberry vinegar flavors thin squid rings and sliced shiitake mushrooms spooned atop rounds of rye toast. For an elegant finish, garnish each canapé with fresh raspberries, mint, and lemon zest.

- 1 **pound cleaned squid mantles (tubes)**
- 5 **large fresh or dried shiitake mushrooms (***each* **2 to 3 inches in diameter)**
- 2 **tablespoons olive oil**
- 1 **cup** *each* **dry white wine and whipping cream**
- 3 **tablespoons raspberry vinegar or lemon juice**
- ½ **teaspoon freshly ground pepper**
  Salt
- 30 **slices cocktail rye bread, lightly toasted**
  Raspberries
  Long, thin shreds of lemon peel
  Fresh mint sprigs

Cut squid mantles crosswise into ⅛- to ¼-inch-thick rings; set aside.

If using dried mushrooms, soak them in cold water to cover until soft (about 30 minutes); drain. Cut off and discard stems of fresh or dried mushrooms; slice caps thinly. Heat oil in a wide frying pan over medium heat. Add mushrooms; cook, stirring, until soft (about 3 minutes). Lift out mushrooms and set aside.

Add wine and cream to pan; bring to a boil, then reduce heat so liquid simmers. Add squid; adjust heat so mixture barely simmers. Cook, stirring occasionally, until squid is tender to bite (5 to 6 minutes); using a slotted spoon, lift out squid and add to mushrooms.

Increase heat to high and bring liquid in pan to a boil; cook, stirring occasionally, until reduced to 1 cup. Add squid and mushrooms to pan, then remove from heat. Blend in vinegar and pepper; season to taste with salt. Spoon an equal amount of the squid mixture onto each toast slice. Garnish with raspberries, lemon peel, and mint sprigs. Serve hot. Makes 2½ dozen appetizers.

Per appetizer: 65 calories, 3 g protein, 5 g carbohydrates, 4 g total fat, 44 mg cholesterol, 49 mg sodium

To Microwave Shrimp

On a flat 10- to 12-inch microwave-safe plate, arrange 1 pound **medium-large raw shrimp** (30 to 35 per lb.), shelled and deveined, if desired, in a single layer with meaty portion toward outside of plate. Cover with heavy-duty plastic wrap. Microwave on **HIGH (100%)** for 4 to 5 minutes, bringing cooked portion toward inside of plate after 2 minutes. Let stand, covered, for 3 to 5 minutes or until shrimp are opaque throughout (cut to test).

Grilled Cheese with Yucatecan Tomato & Shrimp Salsa

Preparation time: About 15 minutes

Cooking time: 12 to 15 minutes

Bubbling hot from the barbecue (or microwave oven), cheese fondue in the style of Mexico's Yucatán is crowned with spicy salsa and tiny shrimp. Crisp tortilla chips make great scoopers for this party favorite.

- 1½ **tablespoons olive oil**
- 1 **large onion, finely chopped**
- 2 **large tomatoes, seeded and chopped**
- ¼ **teaspoon ground cinnamon**
- 4 **to 6 small fresh or canned jalapeño chiles, seeded and finely chopped**
  Salt
- 2 **pounds semisoft mild cheese such as jack, teleme, fontina, or queso asadero**
- 6 **ounces tiny cooked and shelled shrimp**
  Tortilla chips

Heat oil in a wide frying pan over medium-high heat. Add onion and cook, stirring often, until limp (about 5 minutes). Add tomatoes and cinnamon and increase heat to high. Cook, stirring, just until liquid has evaporated (about 2 minutes). Stir in chiles; season to taste with salt. (At this point, you may cover and refrigerate for up to a day.)

Trim and discard wax coating from cheese, if necessary. Cut cheese into ¼-inch-thick slices. In an 8- to 10-inch-wide, 1½- to 2-inch-deep heatproof dish or metal pan, overlap cheese slices to cover dish bottom and extend up sides just to rim. (At this point, you may cover and set aside for up to 4 hours.)

Spoon salsa over center of cheese to make about a 6-inch circle; top with shrimp. Place dish on a grill 4 to 6 inches above a partial bed of medium coals; keep a section of fire grate empty so there's a cool area on grill. Let cheese melt; to be sure cheese isn't scorching on bottom, check frequently by pushing the tip of a knife down into center of dish. If cheese is getting hot too fast, move it to cool area of grill. To eat, scoop melted cheese mixture onto tortilla chips. Makes 12 to 16 appetizer servings.

Per serving: 242 calories, 16 g protein, 2 g carbohydrates, 19 g total fat, 70 mg cholesterol, 330 mg sodium

■ *To Microwave:* Arrange cheese in an 8- to 10-inch microwave-safe casserole or quiche dish. Microwave, uncovered, on **MEDIUM (50%)** for 6 to 8 minutes or until most of cheese is melted, turning dish 3 or 4 times. Top with salsa and shrimp as directed; microwave, uncovered, on **HIGH (100%)** for 2 to 3 more minutes or until cheese is soft enough to scoop. Return to microwave oven briefly once or twice to reheat as necessary.

Shrimp on Cabbage Squares

Preparation time: About 40 minutes

Cooking time: 10 to 12 minutes

Bold with ginger and garlic, a smooth shrimp paste steams atop bite-size squares of napa cabbage in these contemporary Chinese *dim sum.*

> **Fresh Shrimp Paste (recipe follows)**
> 10 to 12 large napa cabbage leaves
> 48 julienne strips thinly sliced cooked ham (*each about 1 inch long*)
> 24 fresh cilantro (coriander) leaves
> Soy sauce

Prepare Fresh Shrimp Paste; set aside.

Cut off leafy portions of cabbage, then cut thick stems into twenty-four 1½-inch squares; reserve leaves and trimmings for other uses. Arrange cabbage squares on a steamer rack set over about 1 inch of water. Cover and bring to a boil over high heat; cook just until cabbage is slightly wilted (about 2 minutes). Drain well.

On each cabbage square, mound about 1½ teaspoons Fresh Shrimp Paste. Lightly press 2 ham strips and a cilantro leaf into each mound. Place

cabbage squares slightly apart on an 11- to 12-inch heatproof plate; cover with plastic wrap. (At this point, you may cover and refrigerate for up to 8 hours.)

Place plate in a steamer basket or on a rack set over 1 inch of boiling water in a wok or deep, wide pan. Cover and steam over high heat until shrimp paste feels firm when lightly pressed (6 to 8 minutes). Serve with soy sauce for dipping. Makes 2 dozen appetizers.

Fresh Shrimp Paste. Shell and devein ½ pound **medium-size raw shrimp** (30 to 50 per lb.). In a food processor, combine shrimp, 2 **egg whites,** 1 tablespoon *each* **dry sherry** and minced **fresh ginger,** 1 clove **garlic** (minced or pressed), 2 teaspoons **cornstarch,** 1 teaspoon **sugar,** ½ teaspoon *each* **salt** and **Oriental sesame oil,** and ⅛ teaspoon **ground white pepper.** Whirl until mixture forms a smooth paste. (Or finely mince shrimp with a knife, then combine with remaining ingredients; beat until well blended and sticky.)

Per appetizer: 18 calories, 2 g protein, 1 g carbohydrates, .39 g total fat, 13 mg cholesterol, 89 mg sodium

■ *To Microwave:* To precook cabbage, place squares in a microwave-safe bowl; cover with heavy-duty plastic wrap. Microwave on **HIGH (100%)** for 2 minutes. Rotate bowl a half-turn, then microwave on **HIGH (100%)** for 1 to 2 more minutes or just until cabbage is slightly wilted. Drain well.

To steam shrimp-topped cabbage squares, place slightly apart on an 11- to 12-inch microwave-safe plate; cover with heavy-duty plastic wrap. Microwave on **HIGH (100%)** for 1½ minutes. Rotate plate a half-turn, then microwave on **HIGH (100%)** for 1½ more minutes or until shrimp paste feels firm when lightly pressed. Let stand for about 5 minutes before serving.

Pictured on facing page

Shrimp Pot Stickers

Preparation time: About 40 minutes

Cooking time: 35 to 40 minutes

Making these classic Chinese appetizers is easy when you use purchased wrappers and shape the dumplings with a pot sticker press. Look for the press in Asian markets and cookware catalogues.

- 1 **pound medium-size raw shrimp (30 to 50 per lb.), shelled and deveined**
- 1 **tablespoon *each* cornstarch and dry sherry**
- 1 **egg**
- 2 **teaspoons *each* soy sauce and minced fresh ginger**
- ¼ **cup *each* thinly sliced green onions (including tops) and finely chopped celery**
- 4 **to 5 dozen pot sticker (*gyoza*) wrappers**
  Salad oil
  About 1½ cups white wine vinegar
  Soy sauce and chili oil

Mince shrimp with a knife (or whirl in a food processor, using short on-off bursts). Transfer to a bowl and mix in cornstarch, sherry, egg, the 2 teaspoons soy sauce, ginger, onions, and celery.

To make each pot sticker, center a wrapper on open pot sticker press; mound 1 teaspoon shrimp filling in center. Moisten edge of wrapper with water; close press, applying pressure to seal edge.

As pot stickers are shaped, place them, pinched sides up, slightly apart on rimmed baking sheets; push down slightly to flatten bottoms so pot stickers sit steadily. Cover with plastic wrap to prevent drying. (At this point, you may refrigerate for up to 4 hours. Or freeze until solid—about 1 hour—then transfer to airtight containers for up to 3 months. Do not thaw before cooking.)

Heat 1 tablespoon salad oil in a wide nonstick frying pan over medium heat. Add 12 to 18 pot stickers, pinched sides up and slightly apart. Cook, uncovered, until bottoms are golden (about 3 minutes). Pour in ½ cup water, reduce heat, cover, and simmer until wrappers look translucent (6 to 8 minutes). Transfer to a warm platter, cover, and keep warm while you cook remaining pot stickers. For each batch of pot stickers, use about 1 tablespoon more salad oil and ½ cup more water.

Serve pot stickers with individual small dipping dishes; into each, pour about 2 tablespoons vinegar, then season to taste with soy sauce and chili oil. Makes 4 to 5 dozen pot stickers.

Per pot sticker: 35 calories, 2 g protein, 4 g carbohydrates, 1 g total fat, 14 mg cholesterol, 22 mg sodium

Pictured on facing page

Sesame-Ginger-Romaine Fish Bundles

Preparation time: About 30 minutes

Cooking time: 8 to 12 minutes

Hot news for summer parties: wrap sesame-, soy-, and ginger-seasoned fish in lettuce, sizzle the bundles on the barbecue, and serve as light and tempting appetizers.

- 16 **green onions (*each* at least 12 inches long), roots trimmed**
- 1½ **pounds boneless and skinless white-fleshed fish fillets, such as orange roughy, flounder, or sole (⅓ to ½ inch thick)**
- 2 **tablespoons *each* minced fresh ginger, lemon juice, and soy sauce**
- 1 **tablespoon Oriental sesame oil or salad oil**
- 6 **large romaine lettuce leaves**
- 12 **slices lemon (*each* ⅛ inch thick)**

In a wide frying pan, bring about 1 inch of water to a boil; immerse 12 of the onions in boiling water until limp (15 to 30 seconds). Drain, immerse in cold water until cool, drain again, and set aside.

Cut remaining 4 onions into 3-inch lengths; split thick ends in half lengthwise. Set aside.

Rinse fish and pat dry. Cut into 12 equal pieces, each about 3 inches square. In a bowl, mix ginger, lemon juice, soy sauce, and sesame oil; add fish and mix lightly to coat. Cut each romaine leaf in half lengthwise along rib; remove and discard ribs.

To assemble each bundle, lay one blanched whole onion out flat. Place one lettuce-leaf half lengthwise down length of onion. Set a piece of fish 2 inches from base of leaf. Top with 3 onion pieces and a lemon slice. Fold base of leaf over top, then roll until leaf is completely wrapped around fish. Center fish bundle, seam side down, on whole onion. Lift ends of onion and tie securely around bundle.

Repeat to make remaining fish bundles. (At this point, you may cover and refrigerate for up to 4 hours.)

To cook, place bundles on a lightly greased grill 3 to 4 inches above a solid bed of hot coals. Cook, turning once, until fish in one of the bundles is just slightly translucent or wet inside; cut in thickest part to test (8 to 12 minutes *total*). Makes 1 dozen appetizers.

Per appetizer: 91 calories, 9 g protein, 2 g carbohydrates, 5 g total fat, 11 mg cholesterol, 209 mg sodium

*Savor the tantalizing tastes of Asia in this collection of
hot morsels. From top: Shrimp Pot Stickers (recipe on
facing page), Sesame-Ginger-Romaine Fish Bundles
(recipe on facing page), and Chinese Crab Claw
Appetizers (recipe on page 25).*

H.B. Little's Codfish Balls

Soaking time: At least 8 hours

Preparation time: About 20 minutes

Cooking time: About 45 minutes

A staple in northern Europe during the Middle Ages, dried salted cod later played an important role in the diet of New Englanders. Still popular today are these classic codfish balls—crusty deep-fried morsels served with a tangy dipping sauce.

Before using dried cod, you'll need to soak it overnight, both to soften it for cooking and to remove some of the salt.

- 1 **box (1 lb.) dried codfish**
- 3 **medium-size russet potatoes**
- 3 **tablespoons butter or margarine**
- 2 **eggs**
- 2 **to 3 tablespoons half-and-half or milk**
  Salt and pepper
  Dipping Sauce (recipe follows)
  Salad oil

Place codfish in a 2- to 3-quart bowl and add enough cold water to cover. Refrigerate for at least 8 hours or until next day, changing water several times. Drain fish, place in a 3- to 4-quart pan, and pour in water to cover. Bring to a boil over high heat; reduce heat, cover, and simmer until fish is soft (3 to 5 minutes). Drain well. Whirl fish in a food processor (or pull apart with your fingers) until finely shredded. Set aside.

While fish is cooking, peel potatoes and cut them into quarters; place in a 3- to 4-quart pan and add 1 inch of water. Bring to a boil over high heat; reduce heat, cover, and boil gently until potatoes are tender when pierced (about 20 minutes). Drain

potatoes well, then mash until free of lumps. Beat in butter, eggs, and shredded fish. Beat in half-and-half, 1 tablespoon at a time, until mixture is cohesive enough to shape into balls. Season to taste with salt and pepper; set aside.

Prepare Dipping Sauce; set aside.

Shape fish mixture into balls about 1½ inches in diameter. In a wide, heavy frying pan, heat 1 inch of oil over medium-high heat to 375°F on a deep-frying thermometer. Add fish balls, a few at a time, and cook until browned on all sides (2 to 3 minutes); adjust heat as necessary to keep oil at 375°F. Lift fish balls out with a slotted spoon, drain on paper towels, and keep warm in a 250° oven until all are cooked.

Offer picks to spear fish balls; dunk into Dipping Sauce to taste before eating. Makes 3½ to 4 dozen appetizers.

Per appetizer: 67 calories, 6 g protein, 2 g carbohydrates, 4 g total fat, 28 mg cholesterol, 676 mg sodium

Dipping Sauce. In a small serving bowl, stir together ½ cup **tomato-based chili sauce** and 1 teaspoon **prepared horseradish**. Makes ½ cup.

Per tablespoon: 18 calories, .42 g protein, 4 g carbohydrates, .05 g total fat, 0 mg cholesterol, 229 mg sodium

Warm Crab Terrine

Preparation time: About 35 minutes

Baking time: 45 to 50 minutes

Cooling time: About 20 minutes

Served barely warm on a bed of crisp greens, slices of this delicately seasoned seafood terrine make an elegant first course.

- ¼ **cup butter or margarine**
- ½ **cup chopped shallots**
- 3 **eggs, separated**
- ½ **cup whipping cream**
- 2 **teaspoons *each* lemon juice and Dijon mustard**
- ¼ **teaspoon salt**
- ⅛ **teaspoon ground white pepper**
- 1 **cup soft bread crumbs**
- ¾ **pound cooked crabmeat**
- ¼ **cup chopped parsley**
  Caper Vinaigrette Dressing (recipe follows)
  Frisée or curly endive, washed and crisped
  Chopped chives and chopped hard-cooked egg

Melt butter in a small frying pan over medium-low heat. Add shallots and cook, stirring often, until soft but not browned (about 5 minutes); remove from heat and set aside.

In a large bowl, beat together egg yolks, cream, lemon juice, mustard, salt, and pepper. Lightly mix in bread crumbs, shallot mixture, crab, and parsley. In another bowl, beat egg whites until stiff but not dry; fold lightly into crab mixture. Spread in a well-greased 4½- by 8½-inch loaf pan.

Bake, uncovered, in a 350° oven until loaf is golden brown and feels just set when lightly touched in center (45 to 50 minutes). Let cool in pan for about 20 minutes. Meanwhile, prepare Caper Vinaigrette Dressing.

Turn terrine out onto a platter. Cut into ½-inch-thick slices and serve slices on a bed of frisée, spooning dressing over them and sprinkling with chives and hard-cooked egg. Makes 6 to 8 first-course servings.

Caper Vinaigrette Dressing. Drain 1½ teaspoons **capers;** set aside. Measure out 1½ teaspoons **caper liquid;** pour into a bowl and mix in 1 tablespoon *each* **red wine vinegar** and **lemon juice,** 1 teaspoon **Dijon mustard,** ¼ teaspoon *each* grated **lemon peel** and **salt,** a pinch of coarsely ground **pepper,** and 1 small clove **garlic,** minced or pressed. Using a fork or whisk, gradually beat in ⅓ cup **olive oil** or salad oil until well combined. Stir in drained capers. Makes about ½ cup.

Per serving: 273 calories, 12 g protein, 6 g carbohydrates, 22 g total fat, 178 mg cholesterol, 512 mg sodium

Pictured on page 23

Chinese Crab Claw Appetizers

Preparation time: About 15 minutes

Cooking time: 12 to 15 minutes

Crab claws provide a convenient handle for these appetizers of crabmeat coated with seafood paste, then deep-fried. Look for the claws (from a variety of crab species) in Asian grocery stores and well-stocked fish markets.

   1 egg white
   ¼ cup thinly sliced green onions (including tops)
   1 tablespoon *each* dry sherry and minced fresh ginger
   2 teaspoons cornstarch
   ¼ teaspoon *each* pepper and Oriental sesame oil
   ¼ pound sole fillets (rinsed and patted dry)
   ¼ pound cooked crabmeat
   12 to 14 cooked crab claws, including pincers (about 1 lb. *total*) with part of shell sawed off, thawed if frozen
       Lime Sauce (recipe follows)
       Salad oil

In a food processor or blender, combine egg white, onions, sherry, ginger, cornstarch, pepper, sesame oil, and sole; whirl until smoothly puréed. Transfer to a bowl and mix in crab. With a spoon, spread an equal portion of crab mixture evenly over meaty portion of each claw. Set prepared claws aside on wax paper. Prepare Lime Sauce; set aside.

In a deep, heavy 2- to 3-quart pan, heat 1½ inches of salad oil to 350°F on a deep-frying thermometer. Cook claws, 3 at a time, until crab mixture is golden brown (3 to 4 minutes). Lift out with a slotted spoon and drain on paper towels; keep warm until all claws are cooked. Serve with Lime Sauce for dipping. Makes 12 to 14 appetizers.

Per appetizer: 72 calories, 7 g protein, .64 g carbohydrates, 4 g total fat, 29 mg cholesterol, 80 mg sodium

Lime Sauce. Mix 3 tablespoons *each* **soy sauce** and **lime juice** and 1 **small fresh hot green chile** (such as jalapeño or serrano), seeded and finely chopped. Makes about 7 tablespoons.

Per tablespoon: 6 calories, .43 g protein, 1 g carbohydrates, .01 g total fat, 0 mg cholesterol, 442 mg sodium

*A Pacific Northwest rendition of French bouillabaisse,
our Puget Sound Seafood Stew (recipe on page 29) is a
sumptuous feast—rockfish, shrimp, mussels, clams, even
fresh crayfish if you can find them. Serve with toasted
French bread and smooth, saffron-tinted Rouille Sauce.*

Soups & Stews

Versatile seafood soups and stews play a pleasant part in many meals. A small bowl of Mussel-Saffron Cream Soup starts dinner with style; Puget Sound Seafood Stew provides a whole meal from just one kettle. Between these extremes, our hot and cold soups and simple to sophisticated stews serve up appetizing answers to that everyday question, "What's for lunch?" . . . or supper, or dinner.

In most cases, we've stated the yields for our recipes as the number of main-dish servings each provides, but there's no reason you can't offer smaller portions as a first course. Let your appetite (and the rest of your menu) be your guide.

Veracruz-style Spicy Snapper Soup

Preparation time: 15 to 20 minutes

Cooking time: 30 to 35 minutes

Gently simmered in a piquant tomato broth, snapper or rockfish stars in a wonderfully warming first course for a chilly night. Pass a basket of hot corn muffins to accompany the soup.

 1 tablespoon olive oil
 1 medium-size onion, finely chopped
 2 cloves garlic, minced or pressed
 ½ teaspoon dry oregano leaves
 ¼ teaspoon cumin seeds, coarsely crushed
 1 bay leaf
 1 or 2 fresh or canned jalapeño chiles, seeded and chopped
 1 small jar (2 oz.) diced pimentos
 1 can (14½ oz.) regular-strength chicken broth
 2¼ cups tomato juice
 1 orange
 ½ pound skinless white-fleshed fish fillets, such as snapper or rockfish
 ¼ cup fresh cilantro (coriander) leaves
   Salt
   Lime wedges

Heat oil in a 2½- to 3-quart pan over medium heat. Add onion, garlic, oregano, and cumin seeds; cook, stirring often, until onion is soft (about 5 minutes). Mix in bay leaf, chiles, pimentos, broth, and tomato juice. Bring to a boil; then reduce heat, cover, and simmer for 20 minutes.

Meanwhile, grate 1 teaspoon peel from orange, then squeeze juice. Set grated peel and juice aside. Rinse fish fillets, pat dry, and cut into bite-size pieces; remove any small bones.

Add fish, orange peel, orange juice, and cilantro to simmering broth. Increase heat to medium, cover, and simmer until fish is just slightly translucent or wet inside; cut in thickest part to test (5 to 7 minutes). Season to taste with salt. Offer lime wedges to squeeze into soup to taste. Makes 4 first-course servings.

Per serving: 148 calories, 13 g protein, 13 g carbohydrates, 6 g total fat, 20 mg cholesterol, 990 mg sodium

■ *To Microwave:* In a 2½- to 3-quart microwave-safe casserole or soup tureen, mix oil, onion, garlic, oregano, and cumin seeds. Microwave, covered, on **HIGH (100%)** for 6 minutes or until onion is soft, stirring 2 or 3 times. Add bay leaf, chiles, pimentos, broth, tomato juice, and orange juice. Microwave, covered, on **HIGH (100%)** for 10 to 12 minutes or until liquid is steaming hot, stirring 2 or 3 times. Add orange peel, fish, and cilantro. Microwave, covered, on **HIGH (100%)** for 3 to 5 minutes or until fish tests done. Season and serve as directed.

Lean Fish &
Pasta Chowder

Preparation time: About 10 minutes

Cooking time: 20 to 25 minutes

Frozen white fish fillets make an impromptu yet pleasing main dish for busy weeknights. Let the fish thaw slightly while you prepare the other ingredients.

 2 tablespoons olive oil
 1 medium-size onion, sliced
 1 large carrot, sliced
 ¼ cup minced parsley
 1 teaspoon dry tarragon
 ¼ teaspoon pepper
 10 to 16 ounces individually frozen (or frozen in a block) white-fleshed fish fillets, such as sole, ocean perch, cod, haddock, or orange roughy, thawed slightly
 2 bottles (8 oz. *each*) clam juice
 1½ cups tomato juice
 ½ cup water
 ⅓ cup dry small seashell-shaped pasta

Heat oil in a 4- to 5-quart pan over medium heat. Add onion, carrot, parsley, tarragon, and pepper; cook, stirring often, until onion is soft but not browned (about 10 minutes). Meanwhile, cut fish into 1-inch chunks; remove any small bones. Set fish aside.

Stir clam juice, tomato juice, water, and pasta into vegetable mixture. Increase heat to high and bring mixture to a boil; then reduce heat, cover, and boil gently for 5 minutes. Add fish, cover, and simmer until fish is just slightly translucent or wet inside; cut in thickest part to test (3 to 5 minutes). Makes 4 servings.

Per serving: 199 calories, 16 g protein, 16 g carbohydrates, 8 g total fat, 34 mg cholesterol, 657 mg sodium

■ *To Microwave:* In a 3½- to 4-quart microwave-safe casserole or tureen, mix oil, onion, carrot, parsley, tarragon, and pepper. Microwave, covered, on **HIGH (100%)** for 7 to 9 minutes or until onion is soft, stirring 2 or 3 times. Stir in clam juice, tomato juice, water, and pasta. Microwave, covered, on **HIGH (100%)** for 12 to 15 minutes or until pasta is nearly tender to bite, stirring twice. Stir in fish; microwave, covered, on **HIGH (100%)** for 2 minutes. Let stand, covered, for 3 minutes.

Doña Elena's Fish Soup

Preparation time: About 25 minutes

Cooking time: 35 to 40 minutes

Fillets of cod or other lean fish poach in this robust, dill-seasoned vegetable soup. Green olives and a little lime juice add tangy accents.

 ¼ cup olive oil or salad oil
    About 1¼ pounds thin-skinned potatoes, diced
 1 large red bell pepper, seeded and diced
 1 medium-size onion, finely chopped
 ¾ cup chopped celery tops
 1 quart regular-strength chicken broth
 1 can (14½ oz.) stewed tomatoes
 ½ cup pitted green olives
 2 pounds skinless lean white-fleshed fish fillets, such as cod, lingcod, or rockfish
 2 tablespoons lime juice
 1 tablespoon chopped fresh dill or 1 teaspoon dry dill weed
 4 cloves garlic, minced or pressed

Heat oil in a 5- to 6-quart pan over medium heat. Add potatoes, bell pepper, onion, and celery; cook, stirring often, until vegetables are lightly browned (15 to 20 minutes). Add broth, tomatoes and their liquid, and olives. Bring to a boil; reduce heat, cover, and boil gently until potatoes are tender when pierced (about 15 minutes).

Meanwhile, rinse fish, pat dry, and cut into 6 to 8 equal pieces; remove any small bones. Add to soup along with lime juice, dill, and garlic. Cover and simmer until fish is just slightly translucent or wet inside; cut in thickest part to test (about 5 minutes). Makes 6 to 8 servings.

Per serving: 265 calories, 23 g protein, 20 g carbohydrates, 10 g total fat, 59 mg cholesterol, 921 mg sodium

Curried Fish Chowder

Preparation time: About 15 minutes

Cooking time: About 30 minutes

Curry powder tints this chowder golden yellow. Hearty with cod or rockfish (or halibut or orange roughy), it's topped with cool yogurt to temper the dried hot chiles that season the broth.

2 tablespoons butter or margarine
1 large onion, finely chopped
2 tablespoons minced fresh ginger
1 clove garlic, minced or pressed
1½ tablespoons curry powder
1½ quarts regular-strength chicken broth
2 medium-size thin-skinned potatoes, diced
1 large carrot, diced
3 strips lemon peel (yellow part only), *each* ½ by 4 inches
2 small dried hot red chiles
1 pound skinless white-fleshed fish fillets, such as cod, rockfish, halibut, or orange roughy
¼ cup thinly sliced green onions (including tops)
1 cup plain yogurt
Lemon wedges

Melt butter in a 5- to 6-quart pan over medium-high heat. Add chopped onion, ginger, and garlic; cook, stirring often, until onion is soft (about 5 minutes). Blend in curry powder; cook, stirring, for 1 minute. Add broth, potatoes, carrot, lemon peel, and chiles. Increase heat to high and bring to a boil. Reduce heat, cover, and boil gently until potatoes are tender when pierced (about 20 minutes).

Meanwhile, rinse fish, pat dry, and cut into ½-inch-square pieces; remove any small bones. Add fish to soup, cover, and simmer until just slightly translucent or wet inside; cut in thickest part to test (2 to 3 minutes). If desired, remove and discard lemon peel and chiles. Sprinkle with 1 tablespoon of the green onions before serving. Offer remaining 3 tablespoons green onions, yogurt, and lemon to add to taste. Makes 4 to 6 servings.

Per serving: 218 calories, 20 g protein, 17 g carbohydrates, 8 g total fat, 39 mg cholesterol, 1,125 mg sodium

Pictured on page 26

Puget Sound Seafood Stew

Preparation time: About 40 minutes

Cooking time: About 35 minutes

Mussels, clams, shrimp, and crayfish (if you can track some down) join chunks of white-fleshed fish in this mouthwatering version of bouillabaisse from the Pacific Northwest.

Rouille Sauce (recipe follows)
½ teaspoon crushed saffron threads
2 tablespoons *each* Pernod and dry vermouth
2 tablespoons olive oil or salad oil
2 large onions, chopped
½ cup chopped parsley
2 large cloves garlic, minced or pressed
6 large tomatoes, peeled, seeded, and cut into wedges
1 tablespoon fennel seeds
1 teaspoon chili powder
2 quarts Fish Stock (page 37)
1 pound skinless lean white-fleshed fish fillets, such as rockfish, cod, or lingcod
12 mussels in shells, prepared (see page 13)
12 medium-size raw shrimp (30 to 50 per lb.), deveined but not shelled
12 medium-size hard-shell clams in shells, suitable for steaming, scrubbed
4 to 12 crayfish, sprayed with cool water (optional)
Sliced French bread, lightly toasted

Prepare Rouille Sauce; set aside. In a bowl, mix saffron, Pernod, and vermouth; set aside.

Heat oil in a 6- to 8-quart pan over medium heat. Add onions and cook, stirring often, until golden brown (about 15 minutes). Stir in saffron mixture, parsley, garlic, tomatoes, fennel seeds, chili powder, and Fish Stock. Bring to a boil; then reduce heat and boil gently, uncovered, for 5 minutes.

Meanwhile, rinse fish, pat dry, and cut into chunks; remove any small bones. Add fish, mussels, shrimp, clams, and crayfish (if used) to soup. Cover and adjust heat so mixture boils very gently; cook until mussels and clams open (12 to 15 minutes).

Ladle seafood and broth into a large tureen or individual wide soup bowls, discarding any unopened clams and mussels. Offer Rouille Sauce to spoon into soup or to spread on bread slices to dunk into broth. Makes 4 to 6 servings.

Per serving: 275 calories, 26 g protein, 22 g carbohydrates, 9 g total fat, 82 mg cholesterol, 890 mg sodium

Rouille Sauce. Using a mortar and pestle or the back of a spoon, grind 2 teaspoons **saffron threads** to a powder; then stir in about 1 teaspoon **olive oil** to make a paste. In blender or food processor, whirl saffron paste, 1 **egg**, 4 cloves **garlic**, ½ teaspoon **paprika**, ¼ teaspoon **crushed red pepper,** and ⅛ teaspoon **ground red pepper** (cayenne) until blended. With motor on high, add 1 cup **olive oil**— a few drops at a time at first, increasing to a steady stream about ¹⁄₁₆ inch wide. If made ahead, cover and refrigerate for up to a week. Makes 1¼ cups.

Per tablespoon: 103 calories, .33 g protein, .30 g carbohydrates, 11 g total fat, 14 mg cholesterol, 4 mg sodium

Tarragon Wine Seafood Chowder

Preparation time: 10 to 15 minutes

Cooking time: About 40 minutes

A touch of tarragon flavors this seafood and potato chowder. Complete a simple yet magnificent menu with a crisp green salad and bread sticks.

- ¼ cup butter or margarine
- 1 large onion, finely chopped
- 1 clove garlic, minced or pressed
- ¼ cup all-purpose flour
- 1 quart regular-strength chicken broth
- 1 cup *each* dry white wine and water
- ¼ teaspoon dry tarragon
- 2 medium-size thin-skinned potatoes, diced
- 12 to 18 small hard-shell clams in shells, suitable for steaming, scrubbed
- 1 pound skinless white-fleshed fish fillets, such as rockfish, cod, or orange roughy
- ½ cup whipping cream
- ¼ pound tiny cooked and shelled shrimp or cooked crabmeat
- Salt and pepper
- 2 tablespoons chopped parsley

Melt butter in a 5- to 6-quart pan over medium-high heat. Add onion and garlic; cook, stirring often, until onion is soft (about 5 minutes). Blend in flour and cook, stirring constantly, until mixture is bubbly. Remove from heat and gradually stir in broth; return to heat and stir in wine, water, and tarragon. Increase heat to high and bring to a boil. Add potatoes, reduce heat, cover, and boil gently until potatoes are tender when pierced (about 20 minutes).

Add clams, cover, and simmer until clams begin to open (5 to 10 minutes). Meanwhile, rinse fish, pat dry, and cut into ½-inch-square pieces; remove any small bones. Add fish to soup, cover, and simmer until just slightly translucent or wet inside; cut in thickest part to test (2 to 3 minutes). Mix in cream and shrimp; cover and simmer until steaming hot (2 to 4 minutes). Season to taste with salt and pepper. Discard any unopened clams. Sprinkle soup with parsley before serving. Makes 6 servings.

Per serving: 320 calories, 26 g protein, 16 g carbohydrates, 17 g total fat, 116 mg cholesterol, 864 mg sodium

---

Pictured on facing page

Cool Sea Salad Soup with Scallops

Preparation time: About 20 minutes

Chilling time: At least 4 hours

Salad merges with soup in this scintillating main dish. Tangy scallop seviche and diced tomatoes are served atop a creamy green purée of cucumbers, watercress, green onions, and yogurt.

- 1 pound bay scallops or sea scallops
- ⅔ cup lemon juice
- 3 medium-size cucumbers
- ⅓ cup firmly packed watercress sprigs
- ⅓ cup thinly sliced green onions (including tops)
- 1 cup plain yogurt
- Salt
- 2 medium-size pear-shaped (Roma-type) tomatoes, diced

If using sea scallops, cut them into ½-inch pieces. Rinse and drain scallops, then place them in a bowl and mix in lemon juice. Cover and refrigerate, stirring occasionally, until scallops are opaque throughout; cut to test (at least 4 hours or until next day). With a slotted spoon, lift out scallops, reserving lemon juice. Cover scallops and return to refrigerator.

Cut off a third of one of the cucumbers; refrigerate cut-off cucumber piece and 4 of the watercress sprigs to use for garnish. Coarsely chop remaining cucumbers.

In a food processor or blender, combine reserved lemon juice, chopped cucumbers, remaining watercress sprigs, onions, and yogurt; whirl until very smoothly puréed. Season to taste with salt. (At this point, you may cover and refrigerate for up to 4 hours.)

To serve, score reserved piece of cucumber with a fork, then thinly slice. Drain any liquid from scallops; stir liquid into cucumber purée. Divide soup among 4 bowls. Top each portion with a fourth each of the scallops, tomatoes, and sliced cucumber. Garnish each serving with a watercress sprig. Makes 4 servings.

Per serving: 181 calories, 24 g protein, 18 g carbohydrates, 2 g total fat, 41 mg cholesterol, 241 sodium

When summer heats up, serve frosty bowls of Cool Sea Salad Soup with Scallops (recipe on facing page). Simple accompaniments suffice—golden corn muffins and tall glasses of iced tea.

Available on any supermarket shelf, canned seafood has meant convenience to generations of cooks. Whether you bring home succulent salmon or briny baby clams, you can turn out a great dish in just a few minutes. And there's no need to limit dependable canned tuna to salads and casseroles—try it with Swiss cheese and fresh broccoli in a puffy, quichelike pie. Even anchovies and smoked oysters—perennial appetizer favorites—show surprising versatility: here, they enliven a vegetable-laden pasta sauce and a quick hot sandwich.

Creamy Salmon Soup

- 3 tablespoons butter or margarine
- ½ teaspoon dry thyme leaves
- ¼ teaspoon dry marjoram leaves
- 1 large onion, finely chopped
- 1 stalk celery, thinly sliced
- 1 green bell pepper, seeded and chopped
- 1 tablespoon tomato paste
- 2 medium-size thin-skinned potatoes, diced
- ¼ teaspoon paprika
- ⅛ teaspoon ground white pepper
- 1 can (14½ oz.) regular-strength chicken broth
- 1 can (15½ oz.) salmon
- 2 cups half-and-half
  Salt

Melt butter in a 3½- to 4-quart pan over medium heat. Add thyme, marjoram, onion, celery, and bell pepper; cook, stirring occasionally, until onion is soft (6 to 8 minutes). Blend in tomato paste. Add potatoes, paprika, pepper, and broth. Bring to a gentle boil; cover and boil gently until potatoes are tender when pierced (about 20 minutes).

Can This Be Canned Fish?

Meanwhile, drain salmon; discard liquid and any large bones. Break salmon into bite-size pieces. Gently stir salmon and half-and-half into soup. Season to taste with salt. Continue to cook just until soup is steaming hot (do not boil). Makes 4 main-dish servings.

Per serving: 445 calories, 26 g protein, 21 g carbohydrates, 29 g total fat, 103 mg cholesterol, 1,082 mg sodium

New Mexican Clam Chowder

Pictured on page 34

- 4 slices bacon
- 2 medium-size onions, finely chopped
- 2 large cans (7 oz. *each*) diced green chiles
- 2 cloves garlic, minced or pressed
- ½ teaspoon ground cumin
- 2 medium-size thin-skinned potatoes, diced
- 2 cans (about 10 oz. *each*) whole baby clams
- 1 quart milk
  Condiments: Sour cream, prepared green or red chile salsa, tortilla or corn chips

In a 4- to 5-quart pan, cook bacon over medium heat until crisp. Lift out, drain, crumble, and set aside; reserve drippings in pan.

To drippings, add onions, chiles, garlic, and cumin; cook, stirring, until onions are soft (about 5 minutes). Add potatoes and juice from clams. Bring to a gentle boil; cover and boil gently until potatoes are tender when pierced (about 20 minutes). Add milk and drained clams; heat, stirring occasionally, until soup is steaming hot (do not boil). Serve bacon and condiments of your choice in separate bowls to add to soup to taste. Makes 4 or 5 servings.

Per serving: 347 calories, 19 g protein, 28 g carbohydrates, 18 g total fat, 76 mg cholesterol, 1,355 mg sodium

Clam Soufflé

- 2 cans (6½ oz. *each*) minced clams
- 3 tablespoons butter or margarine
- 2 tablespoons thinly sliced green onion (including tops)
- 3 tablespoons all-purpose flour
- ¼ teaspoon *each* pepper and ground nutmeg
- 6 eggs, separated
- 2 tablespoons minced parsley
- 1 small jar (2 oz.) diced pimentos, drained

Drain juice from clams into a measuring cup; add water, if needed, to make 1 cup. Set clams and juice aside.

Melt butter in a medium-size frying pan over medium heat; add onion and cook, stirring often, until limp (2 to 3 minutes). Blend in flour, pepper, and nutmeg; cook, stirring, for 1 minute. Remove from heat and gradually stir in clam juice; return to heat and continue to cook, stirring, until sauce boils and thickens. Remove from heat.

In a large bowl, beat egg yolks until blended. Using a wire whisk, gradually blend in sauce; stir in drained clams, parsley, and pimentos.

In another bowl, beat egg whites with an electric mixer until they hold soft, moist peaks. Fold half the beaten whites into clam mixture; then fold in remaining whites. Pour mixture into a greased 2-quart soufflé dish.

Bake in a 350° oven until soufflé is well browned and feels firm when lightly tapped (about 35 minutes). Serve at once. Makes 4 servings.

Per serving: 270 calories, 17 g protein, 9 g carbohydrates, 18 g total fat, 464 mg cholesterol, 721 mg sodium

Hot Smoked Oyster & Tomato Sandwiches

4 **English muffins, split**
2 **tablespoons butter or margarine, at room temperature**
1 **teaspoon Dijon mustard**
8 **tomato slices (*each* about ¼ inch thick)**
1 **can (3¾ oz.) small smoked oysters, drained well**
1 **cup (4 oz.) shredded Swiss cheese**

Toast English muffins. Meanwhile, blend butter and mustard. Spread split sides of muffins with butter mixture. Arrange on a baking sheet in a single layer, buttered sides up. Top each half with a tomato slice. Arrange oysters over tomatoes. Sprinkle evenly with cheese:

Broil about 4 inches below heat until cheese is melted and lightly browned (about 3 minutes). Serve hot. Makes 4 servings (2 halves each).

Per serving: 322 calories, 15 g protein, 30 g carbohydrates, 16 g total fat, 65 mg cholesterol, 509 mg sodium

Anchovy & Eggplant Pasta

¼ **cup olive oil**
½ **teaspoon dry oregano leaves**
1 **small eggplant (about ½ lb.), unpeeled, diced**
3 **cloves garlic, minced or pressed**
1 **can (about 1 lb.) diced tomatoes packed in juice**
½ **cup dry red wine**
¼ **cup oil-cured olives**
1 **can (2 oz.) caper-stuffed rolled anchovies, drained well**
2 **slender medium-size zucchini (4 to 6 oz. *total*), diced**
Freshly ground black pepper
12 **ounces dry spaghettini or vermicelli**
Grated Parmesan cheese

Heat oil in a wide frying pan over medium heat. Add oregano and eggplant; cook, stirring, until eggplant is lightly browned. Add garlic, tomatoes and their juice, wine, and olives. Bring to a boil; then reduce heat, cover, and simmer until eggplant is tender to bite (about 15 minutes). Uncover, stir in anchovies, increase heat to medium, and bring to a boil. Boil gently, stirring occasionally, until sauce is thick (8 to 10 minutes). Stir zucchini into sauce and cook, stirring, until tender-crisp to bite (2 to 3 minutes). Season sauce to taste with pepper.

While sauce is cooking, in a 5½- to 6-quart pan, cook spaghettini in 4 quarts of boiling water just until tender to bite (about 10 minutes); or cook according to package directions. Drain well and arrange on a warm platter; top with sauce, then mix lightly. Offer cheese to add to taste. Makes 4 to 6 servings.

Per serving: 357 calories, 11 g protein, 50 g carbohydrates, 13 g total fat, 4 mg cholesterol, 625 mg sodium

Tuna & Cheese Pie

3 **eggs**
3 **green onions (including tops), thinly sliced**
1 **cup half-and-half**
1 **clove garlic, minced or pressed**
2 **cups (8 oz.) shredded Swiss or jack cheese**
1 **cup chopped fresh broccoli flowerets and tender stems**
Salt and pepper
2 **cans (6½ oz. *each*) chunk-style tuna or 1 can (15½ oz.) salmon, drained and flaked**
1 **(9-inch) pie shell, baked until barely golden**

In a large bowl, beat eggs, onions, half-and-half, and garlic until blended. Mix in cheese and broccoli; season to taste with salt and pepper.

Arrange tuna in a layer in pie shell, mounding it slightly in center. Spoon egg mixture over tuna.

Bake pie on bottom rack of a 350° oven until filling is puffed and lightly browned (about 50 minutes). Let stand for 5 to 10 minutes, then cut into wedges to serve. Makes 6 servings.

Per serving: 506 calories, 34 g protein, 18 g carbohydrates, 33 g total fat, 197 mg cholesterol, 541 mg sodium

Seafood in the Southwest? Here's how it might show up in Santa Fe. Robust New Mexican Clam Chowder (recipe on page 32) features green chiles in the broth, salsa and corn chips to enjoy on top or alongside.

Steamed Clams in Orange-Leek Broth

Preparation time: 10 to 12 minutes

Cooking time: About 25 minutes

Sautéed leeks and clams combine in a fennel-seasoned tomato broth made tangy with plenty of fresh orange juice. Garnish each serving with orange slices, if you like.

- 3 large leeks (about 1 lb. *total*)
- 2 tablespoons butter or margarine
- 2 strips orange peel (orange part only), *each ½ by 3 inches*
- 1 cup orange juice
- 1 can (14½ oz.) pear-shaped tomatoes
- 1 can (14½ oz.) regular-strength chicken broth
- 1¼ cups water
- ½ teaspoon fennel seeds, crushed
- 36 small hard-shell clams in shells, suitable for steaming, scrubbed
  Orange slices (optional)

Trim and discard roots and dark green tops of leeks. Split leeks in half lengthwise and rinse well; thinly slice crosswise.

Melt butter in a 5- to 6-quart pan over medium heat. Add leeks and cook, stirring often, until limp (about 7 minutes). Add orange peel, orange juice, tomatoes (break up with a spoon) and their liquid, broth, water, and fennel seeds. Bring to a boil, stirring occasionally; reduce heat to low, cover, and simmer for 10 minutes.

Increase heat to medium-high. When mixture comes to a boil, add clams. Reduce heat to medium-low, cover, and simmer until clams open (5 to 7 minutes).

With a slotted spoon, lift clams from pan and transfer to individual wide soup bowls; discard any unopened clams. Ladle broth over clams in bowls. Garnish with orange slices, if desired. Makes 4 servings.

Per serving: 247 calories, 20 g protein, 23 g carbohydrates, 8 g total fat, 61 mg cholesterol, 767 mg sodium

Clam Paella for Two

Preparation time: 10 to 12 minutes

Cooking time: 25 to 30 minutes

Unlike more traditional versions of paella, this seafood variation cooks quickly—either on the range top or in the microwave oven. Accompany with hot garlic bread.

- 1 tablespoon olive oil
- 1 clove garlic, minced or pressed
- ¼ teaspoon ground turmeric
- ⅔ cup long-grain white rice
- 2 tablespoons finely chopped parsley
- ½ cup cherry tomatoes, cut into halves
- ⅔ cup dry white wine
- ¾ cup regular-strength chicken broth or bottled clam juice
- 24 small hard-shell clams in shells, suitable for steaming, scrubbed

Heat oil in a wide frying pan over medium heat. Add garlic, turmeric, and rice. Cook, stirring often, until rice begins to look opaque (3 to 5 minutes). Mix in parsley, cherry tomatoes, wine, and broth. Reduce heat to low, cover, and simmer for 15 minutes.

Arrange clams over rice. Cover and cook until clams open and rice is tender to bite (8 to 10 minutes). Discard any unopened clams. Makes 2 servings.

Per serving: 446 calories, 29 g protein, 59 g carbohydrates, 10 g total fat, 61 mg cholesterol, 490 mg sodium

■ *To Microwave:* Omit oil. In a shallow 2-quart microwave-safe casserole, stir together garlic, turmeric, rice, parsley, cherry tomatoes, wine, and ⅔ cup of the broth. Cover loosely with heavy-duty plastic wrap and microwave on **HIGH (100%)**, stirring 3 or 4 times, for 15 to 20 minutes or until rice is tender to bite and liquid is absorbed. If necessary, add more broth to keep rice moist.

Arrange clams around edge of casserole. Cover loosely with another piece of heavy-duty plastic wrap and microwave on **HIGH (100%)** for 4 to 6 minutes or until clams open.

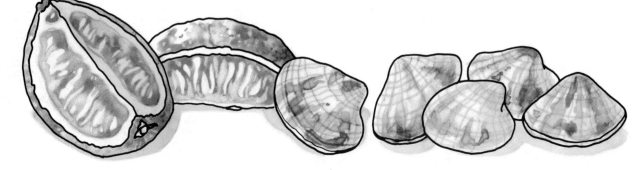

Mussel-Saffron Cream Soup

Preparation time: 15 to 20 minutes

Cooking time: 12 to 15 minutes

On the Atlantic coast of France between Brittany and Bordeaux lies the medieval seaport of La Rochelle, home of this luxurious saffron-scented mussel soup. The soup's French name, *mouclade*, derives from a regional word for "mussel."

- 3 **pounds mussels in shells**
- 2 **cups dry white wine**
- 2 **parsley sprigs**
- 1 **bay leaf**
- ⅛ **teaspoon whole white peppercorns**
- ⅛ **teaspoon crushed saffron threads**
- 3 **tablespoons butter or margarine**
- ⅓ **cup chopped shallots**
- 1 **tablespoon all-purpose flour**
- 2 **egg yolks**
- 1 **teaspoon Dijon mustard**
- 1 **cup whipping cream**
- 2 **tablespoons lemon juice**
  Salt

Prepare mussels (see page 13). In a 4- to 5-quart pan, combine wine, parsley sprigs, bay leaf, and peppercorns. Add mussels; cover and cook over medium-high heat just until shells open (about 5 minutes). Remove from heat.

Remove mussels from pan, reserving cooking liquid. Discard any unopened mussels. Then remove and discard top shells from remaining mussels; place mussels on half shells in a serving bowl or tureen. Cover and keep warm.

Line a wire strainer with a double thickness of dampened cheesecloth; set strainer over a bowl. Pour cooking liquid through cheesecloth; discard cheesecloth. In a small bowl, mix about 2 tablespoons of the hot strained liquid with saffron and set aside to steep.

Rinse cooking pan to remove any bits of grit or shell. Place butter in pan over medium heat; when butter is melted, add shallots and cook, stirring often, until soft but not browned (about 3 minutes). Stir in flour and cook until bubbly. Remove from heat and gradually blend in saffron mixture and strained cooking liquid. Return to heat; cook, stirring, until liquid begins to boil.

In a bowl, beat egg yolks, mustard, cream, and lemon juice until blended. Gradually blend in about ½ cup of the hot liquid; then, using a wire whisk, stir egg mixture back into hot liquid in pan. Cook, stirring constantly, until steaming hot (do not boil). Season to taste with salt; pour over mussels in bowl or tureen. Ladle mussels and soup into individual bowls. Makes 4 first-course servings.

Per serving: 392 calories, 15 g protein, 11 g carbohydrates, 32 g total fat, 253 mg cholesterol, 442 mg sodium

Curry-spiced Steamed Mussels

Preparation time: 30 minutes

Cooking time: About 20 minutes

Mussels steamed in a spicy tomato broth make a marvelous meal. Serve with warm corn bread and cold beer.

- ¼ **cup butter or margarine**
- 1 **large onion, chopped**
- 3 **large cloves garlic, minced or pressed**
- ½ **teaspoon *each* ground cumin, ground turmeric, and crushed red pepper**
- ¼ **teaspoon *each* ground cloves and black pepper**
- 2 **large tomatoes, peeled, seeded, and finely chopped**
- 1⅓ **cups water**
- 3 **to 4 pounds mussels in shells, prepared (see page 13)**
- 3 **tablespoons lemon juice**
  About 1 cup fresh cilantro (coriander) leaves

Melt butter in a 5- to 6-quart pan over medium heat. Add onion and garlic; cook, stirring often, until onion is soft (about 5 minutes). Stir in cumin, turmeric, red pepper, cloves, and black pepper. Cook, stirring, until spices are aromatic (about 3 minutes). Stir in tomatoes and cook for about 2 more minutes. Add water and mussels.

Cover and cook until mussels open (5 to 7 minutes). With a slotted spoon, lift mussels from pan and transfer to individual wide soup bowls; discard any unopened mussels. Ladle broth over mussels. Drizzle each serving with lemon juice and garnish with cilantro. Makes 4 servings.

Per serving: 225 calories, 13 g protein, 12 g carbohydrates, 14 g total fat, 59 mg cholesterol, 411 mg sodium

Shrimp & Rice Chowder

Preparation time: 10 to 15 minutes

Cooking time: About 35 minutes

Jalapeño-hot, this sturdy chowder is packed with tiny peas, shrimp, and rice. Add a squeeze of fresh lime juice to taste.

 2 fresh jalapeño chiles (*each* about 3 inches long)
 2 tablespoons salad oil
 1 large onion, finely chopped
 2 cloves garlic, minced or pressed
 ½ teaspoon cumin seeds
 1½ quarts regular-strength chicken broth
 ⅔ cup short-grain rice (such as pearl)
 3 medium-size pear-shaped (Roma-type) tomatoes, finely chopped
 1 package (10 oz.) frozen tiny peas, thawed
 1 pound tiny cooked and shelled shrimp
 1 large lime, cut into wedges

Cut one of the chiles in half lengthwise; thinly slice remaining chile and set aside.

Heat oil in a 5- to 6-quart pan over medium-high heat. Add onion, garlic, cumin seeds, and 1 or 2 chile halves (to taste). Cook, stirring often, until onion is soft (about 5 minutes). Add broth and rice. Increase heat to high and bring to a boil. Reduce heat, cover, and simmer until rice is very tender to bite (20 to 25 minutes).

Add tomatoes, peas, and all but ½ cup of the shrimp. Simmer, uncovered, until hot (2 to 3 minutes). Remove and discard chile halves. Ladle chowder into wide soup bowls; spoon some of the reserved ½ cup shrimp into each. Garnish with lime wedges and chile slices. Makes 6 servings.

Per serving: 285 calories, 23 g protein, 31 g carbohydrates, 8 g total fat, 148 mg cholesterol, 1,245 mg sodium

Burmese Vegetable & Shrimp Soup

Preparation time: About 25 minutes

Soaking time: About 20 minutes

Cooking time: About 15 minutes

Indian, Thai, and Chinese influences are all apparent in this Burmese-style shrimp soup. Look in Oriental markets for the fish sauce and dried black fungus, often sold as cloud ears or tree ears.

 ½ cup dried black fungus (cloud ears)
 7 cups regular-strength chicken broth
 3 cloves garlic, minced or pressed
 3 tablespoons Oriental fish sauce (*nam pla* or *nuoc nam*) or soy sauce
 1 teaspoon pepper
 2 cups thinly sliced small pattypan squash
 2 cups finely shredded cabbage
 1 pound large raw shrimp (under 30 per lb.), shelled and deveined

In a small bowl, soak fungus in warm water to cover until soft and pliable (about 20 minutes). Loosen any grit with your fingers. Lift fungus out of water; cut out and discard any hard, knobby pieces. Rinse fungus, pat dry, and cut into strips about ⅓ inch wide.

Meanwhile, in a 5- to 6-quart pan, combine broth, garlic, fish sauce, and pepper; bring to a boil over high heat. Reduce heat, cover, and simmer for 10 minutes. Add fungus, squash, cabbage, and shrimp. Cover and simmer until shrimp are opaque throughout (cut to test) and squash is tender-crisp to bite (about 4 minutes). Makes 6 servings.

Per serving: 178 calories, 18 g protein, 11 g carbohydrates, 5 g total fat, 93 mg cholesterol, 1,269 mg sodium

Fish Stock

Homemade fish broth adds extra-fresh flavor to your seafood soups and stews. Use it in place of clam juice or chicken broth in the recipes in this chapter, or wherever Fish Stock is specified.

Thoroughly rinse 2 to 3 pounds **fish heads and carcasses** (do not use fish entrails, gills, or pieces of skin), then break into pieces. (You may also use shrimp or crab shells.) In a 6- to 8-quart pan, combine rinsed fish trimmings with 1 large **onion,** chopped; 1 **carrot,** sliced; ½ cup chopped **parsley;** 1 **bay leaf;** 1 cup **dry white wine** or 3 tablespoons lemon juice; and 2 quarts **water.** Bring to a boil, skimming off any scum from surface. Reduce heat, cover, and simmer for 45 minutes. Strain; discard fish trimmings and seasonings. If made ahead, cover and refrigerate for up to 3 days or freeze for up to 3 months. Makes about 2 quarts.

Vietnamese Summer Soup

Pictured on facing page

Preparation time: About 25 minutes

Soaking & standing time: 30 minutes

Cooking time: 25 to 30 minutes

Shrimp and meaty crab claws are tempting discoveries for diners in this light, gingered broth. Dress up the soup with condiments of your choice: crisp-fried onion rings, hot chile flakes, and fresh lime juice.

> Crisp-fried Onions (recipe follows)
> 2 ounces rice sticks (*mai fun*), broken into 3-inch pieces
> 1½ quarts regular-strength chicken broth
> 1 tablespoon *each* finely chopped fresh ginger and Vietnamese fish sauce (*nuoc nam*)
> ½ pound medium-large raw shrimp (30 to 35 per lb.), shelled and deveined
> ½ pound cooked crab claws (including pincers) with part of shell sawed off, thawed if frozen; or ½ pound medium-large raw shrimp (30 to 35 per lb.), shelled and deveined
> ¼ cup thinly sliced green onions (including tops)
> 1 lime or lemon, cut into wedges
> Crushed red pepper

Prepare Crisp-fried Onions and set aside.

Soak rice sticks in water to cover until limp (about 20 minutes); stir to separate noodles.

In a 5- to 6-quart pan, combine broth, ginger, and fish sauce; bring to a boil over high heat. Drain noodles and add them to broth along with shrimp and crab claws; cover and remove from heat. Let stand until shrimp are opaque throughout; cut to test (about 10 minutes). Stir in onions.

Pour soup into a tureen or individual bowls. Offer Crisp-fried Onions, lime wedges, and red pepper to add to taste. Makes 4 or 5 servings.

Per serving: 154 calories, 16 g protein, 13 g carbohydrates, 4 g total fat, 80 mg cholesterol, 1,328 mg sodium

Crisp-fried Onions. Thinly slice 2 medium-size **onions;** separate into rings. Measure ⅓ to ½ cup **all-purpose flour** into a bag. Add onions, about half at a time; shake to coat lightly with flour. In a deep, heavy 2½- to 3-quart pan, heat 1½ inches of **salad oil** to 300°F on a deep-frying thermometer. Cook onions, about a fourth at a time, stirring often, until golden (about 5 minutes); adjust heat as necessary to keep oil at 300°F.

Lift out onions with a slotted spoon and drain on paper towels. If made ahead, cover airtight and store at room temperature for up to 3 days. Serve at room temperature or reheated. To reheat, spread out in a shallow baking pan; heat in a 350° oven for 2 to 3 minutes. Makes about 3½ cups.

Per ½ cup: 84 calories, .99 g protein, 7 g carbohydrates, 6 g total fat, 0 mg cholesterol, .75 mg sodium

Chinese Chicken & Shrimp Soup

Preparation time: About 25 minutes

Cooking time: About 5 minutes

Present this delicate but nourishing soup as the first course of an Asian dinner, or as a light supper all on its own.

> 1½ quarts regular-strength chicken broth
> 2 tablespoons finely chopped fresh ginger
> 2 to 3 teaspoons soy sauce
> 1 whole chicken breast (about 1 lb.), skinned, boned, split, and cut into ½-inch cubes
> ½ pound mushrooms, sliced
> 3 cups thinly sliced bok choy
> 1 cup diced firm tofu (bean curd)
> ½ cup sliced green onions (including tops)
> ½ pound tiny cooked and shelled shrimp
> ¼ cup chopped fresh cilantro (coriander)
> Ground red pepper (cayenne) or chili oil (optional)

In a 4- to 5-quart pan, combine broth, ginger, and soy sauce. Bring to a boil over high heat; add chicken, mushrooms, bok choy, tofu, and onions. Cook, uncovered, until chicken is no longer pink in center; cut to test (about 2 minutes).

Remove from heat and stir in shrimp and cilantro. Season to taste with red pepper, if desired. Makes 4 main-dish or 6 first-course servings.

Per main-dish serving: 306 calories, 45 g protein, 11 g carbohydrates, 11 g total fat, 153 mg cholesterol, 1,899 mg sodium

■ *To Microwave:* Combine broth, ginger, soy sauce, mushrooms, tofu, and onions in a 3½- to 4-quart microwave-safe casserole. Microwave, covered, on **HIGH (100%)** for 10 to 12 minutes or until broth is steaming hot, stirring once or twice. Stir in chicken and bok choy, cover, and microwave on **HIGH (100%)** for 5 to 8 minutes or until chicken tests done and broth begins to boil. Add shrimp and cilantro, then cover and let stand for 2 minutes before serving. Season as directed.

*Laden with shrimp and crab claws, Vietnamese Summer
Soup (recipe on facing page) gets dressed up at the table
with your choice of condiments: crisp onion rings, fiery
crushed chiles, or a squeeze of tart lime juice.*

Oyster & Artichoke Stew

Preparation time: About 1 hour

Cooking time: About 1¼ hours

This soup celebrates two "luxury" foods—oysters and fresh artichokes—and makes the most of both. Preparation takes time, but the exquisite result is worth it.

- 4 **medium-size artichokes (***each* **about 3 inches in diameter)**
- 2 **quarts water**
- ¾ **teaspoon** *each* **dry thyme leaves and ground nutmeg**
- ¼ **cup butter or margarine**
- ½ **cup** *each* **thinly sliced green onions (including tops) and finely chopped parsley**
- 2 **large cloves garlic, minced or pressed**
- ¼ **to ½ teaspoon ground red pepper (cayenne)**
- 3 **bottles (8 oz.** *each***) clam juice**
- 2 **cups water**
- 24 **medium-size Pacific or Eastern oysters in shells (***each* **about 4 inches long), scrubbed**
- 1 **cup whipping cream**

Rinse artichokes, then pull off and discard tough outer leaves. In a 5- to 6-quart pan, combine artichokes, the 2 quarts water, and ½ teaspoon *each* of the thyme and nutmeg. Bring to a boil over high heat; partially cover and boil until artichoke bottoms are very tender when pierced (about 45 minutes). Drain.

When artichokes are cool enough to handle, pull off leaves. Scrape soft pulp from leaves into pan; discard leaves after scraping. Scrape out and discard fuzzy centers of artichoke bottoms; cut off stems and place in pan with pulp from leaves. Set bottoms aside.

To pulp and stems in pan, add butter, onions, parsley, garlic, remaining ¼ teaspoon *each* thyme and nutmeg, and red pepper. Place over medium heat and stir until butter is melted. Add clam juice and the 2 cups water. Increase heat to high and bring mixture to a boil. Reduce heat, cover, and simmer for 15 minutes.

Whirl artichoke mixture, about a third at a time, in a blender or food processor until puréed. Pour purée through a fine wire strainer into a large bowl to remove any fibers.

Rinse pan, then return strained artichoke broth to it; bring to a boil over high heat. Add oysters, reduce heat to medium-low, cover, and boil very gently just until oysters open slightly (5 to 10 minutes). Lift out oysters as they open, draining juices into pan.

Holding oysters carefully to protect your hands, pry off and discard tops of shells. Place 6 oysters on the half shell in each of 4 wide soup bowls; keep warm.

Stir cream and artichoke bottoms into broth; bring to a simmer. To each bowl, add an artichoke bottom and a fourth of the broth; take care to avoid ladling out any bits of oyster shell from bottom of pan. Makes 4 servings.

Per serving: 413 calories, 12 g protein, 22 g carbohydrates, 33 g total fat, 144 mg cholesterol, 723 mg sodium

Avocado & Crab Bisque

Preparation time: 10 minutes

Cooking time: 25 to 30 minutes

Transform humble potato soup into a stylish bisque with the elegant additions of cream, crabmeat, and diced avocado.

- 4 **slices bacon, diced**
- ¼ **cup thinly sliced green onions (including tops)**
- 1 **medium-size thin-skinned potato, peeled and diced**
- 1 **bottle (8 oz.) clam juice**
- 1 **can (14½ oz.) regular-strength chicken broth**
- 1 **large soft-ripe avocado**
- ½ **cup whipping cream or half-and-half**
- ¼ **to ½ pound cooked crabmeat**
   Paprika and freshly ground pepper

In a 2- to 3-quart pan, cook bacon over medium heat until crisp. Lift out, drain, and set aside. Discard all but 1 tablespoon drippings. Add onions to drippings and cook, stirring often, until limp (2 to 3 minutes). Add potato, clam juice, and broth. Bring to a boil; then reduce heat, cover, and boil gently until potato is very tender when pierced (10 to 15 minutes).

Meanwhile, pit, peel, and dice avocado; set aside. Add cream and crab to potato mixture; stir often until soup is steaming hot. Stir in avocado and bacon; remove from heat. Sprinkle each serving with paprika and pepper. Makes 3 or 4 servings.

Per serving: 328 calories, 12 g protein, 15 g carbohydrates, 26 g total fat, 69 mg cholesterol, 780 mg sodium

Fresh Corn & Seafood Soup

Preparation time: 25 to 30 minutes

Cooking time: About 25 minutes

This light soup exemplifies the new Australian cooking style, with bold Southeast Asian flavors improving upon a blander British base. Serve it as a first course—perhaps before a chicken and vegetable stir-fry—or as a light meal.

Curried Coconut (recipe follows)
2 tablespoons **salad oil**
5 cloves **garlic**, thinly sliced
10 medium-size **shallots** (about ½ lb. *total*), thinly sliced
2 tablespoons **minced fresh ginger**
2 quarts **regular-strength chicken broth**
2 tablespoons **Oriental fish sauce** (*nam pla* or *nuoc nam*) or **soy sauce**
2 cups **fresh corn** cut from cob
1 or 2 **fresh jalapeño or serrano chiles**, seeded and cut into small slivers
¼ pound *each* **cooked crabmeat** and **tiny cooked and shelled shrimp**
1 cup **fresh cilantro (coriander) sprigs**

Prepare Curried Coconut and set aside.

Heat oil in a 5- to 6-quart pan over medium heat. Add garlic, shallots, and ginger; cover and cook, stirring once or twice, until shallots begin to soften (about 5 minutes). Then uncover and continue to cook, stirring often, until shallots are deep golden (about 5 more minutes).

Add broth, fish sauce, corn, and chiles. Increase heat to high and bring mixture to a boil. Reduce heat, cover, and simmer until corn is tender to bite (5 to 10 minutes). Mix in crab, shrimp, and ½ cup of the cilantro sprigs; heat through. Offer Curried Coconut and remaining ½ cup cilantro sprigs to add to taste. Makes 5 or 6 servings.

Per serving: 213 calories, 14 g protein, 21 g carbohydrates, 9 g total fat, 56 mg cholesterol, 1,448 mg sodium

Curried Coconut. Heat 1 tablespoon **salad oil** in a wide frying pan over medium heat. All at once, add 1 teaspoon *each* **ground coriander** and **cumin seeds** and ½ teaspoon *each* **ground ginger** and **ground turmeric**; stir for 30 seconds. Add 1 cup **unsweetened large-flaked or shredded dry coconut**; stir until edges of coconut flakes are golden (about 3 minutes). Makes 1 cup.

Per tablespoon: 35 calories, .31 g protein, 1 g carbohydrates, 3 g total fat, 0 mg cholesterol, 2 mg sodium

Cracked Crab in Spicy Broth

Preparation time: About 5 minutes

Cooking time: About 15 minutes

Cracked crab in a highly seasoned broth makes a deliciously messy meal for two. Serve with lots of crusty bread and a stack of oversize paper napkins.

1 tablespoon **olive oil or salad oil**
1 medium-size **onion**, chopped
1 clove **garlic**, minced or pressed
1 teaspoon **dry mustard**
1 tablespoon *each* **Worcestershire** and **vinegar** ⟋ *salad*
½ teaspoon **dry thyme leaves**
2 tablespoons **soy sauce**
2 cups **water**
2 drops **liquid smoke** (optional)
1 **cooked large Dungeness crab** (about 2½ lbs.), cleaned and cracked

Heat oil in a wide frying pan over medium heat; add onion and garlic. Cook, stirring often, until onion is soft (about 5 minutes). Stir in mustard, Worcestershire, vinegar, thyme, and soy sauce. Add water and liquid smoke (if used). Bring to a boil; then reduce heat and simmer, uncovered, for 5 minutes.

Add crab and cook until heated through (about 5 minutes). Divide crab between 2 wide soup bowls; ladle broth over crab. Makes 2 servings.

Per serving: 238 calories, 30 g protein, 7 g carbohydrates, 10 g total fat, 136 mg cholesterol, 1,493 mg sodium

■ *To Microwave:* In a 3-quart microwave-safe casserole, mix oil, onion, and garlic. Microwave, covered, on **HIGH (100%)** for 5 minutes or until onion is soft, stirring 2 or 3 times. Add mustard, Worcestershire, vinegar, thyme, and soy sauce. Stir in water and liquid smoke (if used). Microwave, covered, on **HIGH (100%)** for 6 to 8 minutes or until liquid begins to boil at edges of casserole. Add crab and microwave, covered, on **HIGH (100%)** for 3 minutes; let stand for 2 minutes, then serve as directed.

For a tantalizing taste of the tropics, bring on Hawaiian Fish & Papaya Salad (recipe on facing page). The creamy dressing tops steeped fish fillets and fruit on a spinach-lined platter.

42

Salads

Scatter a few tiny shrimp over a crisp green salad, and it immediately becomes more attractive to both eye and palate. And that's just one of the countless ways seafood can contribute to salads. Steep fresh fish to show off in imaginative combinations of fruit and greens, as in Hawaiian Fish & Papaya Salad. Or offer tender shrimp in new surroundings—alongside juicy Asian pears, for example. For a strikingly original hot-and-cold first course, spoon poached mussels in warm wine dressing over chilled mustard greens. Let this chapter introduce you to a whole range of appealing seafood salads, from simple coleslaw to a shimmering, sophisticated aspic of halibut and salmon.

Pictured on facing page
Hawaiian Fish & Papaya Salad

Preparation time: 35 to 40 minutes

Cooling time: At least 20 minutes

Cooking time: 8 to 10 minutes

Imparting a sweet-tart taste of the tropics to this salad of spinach, fruit, and cold steeped fish is a creamy dressing made with toasted coconut.

- 4 **skinless white-fleshed fish fillets, such as orange roughy, snapper, tilapia, or mahi mahi (3 to 4 oz. *each*)**
- **Toasted Coconut Dressing (recipe follows)**
- 4 **teaspoons lumpfish caviar (optional)**
- ¾ **pound spinach, rinsed well**
- 2 **stalks celery, thinly sliced**
- 1 **small mild red onion, thinly sliced**
- 1 **large papaya or 2 medium-size mangoes**

In a 3- to 4-quart pan, bring 2 quarts of water to a rolling boil over high heat. Rinse and drain fish; if fillets are under ½ inch thick, fold in half to cook. Remove pan from heat and quickly immerse fish in water. Cover pan tightly and let stand until fish is just slightly translucent or wet inside; cut in thickest part to test (about 4 minutes). With a slotted spatula, carefully lift out fish and let cool for at least 20 minutes. Meanwhile, prepare Toasted Coconut Dressing and set aside.

If using caviar, place in a fine wire strainer and rinse under cold running water. Drain well; set aside. Pat spinach dry, remove stems, and tear into bite-size pieces if necessary; mix lightly with celery and onion. Peel and halve papaya, remove seeds, and cut fruit into ¼-inch-thick slices. (Or peel mangoes, then cut fruit from pit in ¼-inch-thick slices.)

Line a platter with spinach mixture; top with fish. Arrange papaya slices around fish. Spoon a little Toasted Coconut Dressing over each fish fillet. Garnish with caviar, if desired. Pass remaining dressing to add to taste. Makes 4 servings.

Per serving: 151 calories, 20 g protein, 13 g carbohydrates, 2 g total fat, 27 mg cholesterol, 115 mg sodium

Toasted Coconut Dressing. Toast 1 cup **sweetened flaked coconut** or unsweetened shredded dry coconut in a wide frying pan over medium-high heat until golden brown (3 to 5 minutes), stirring often. Remove from heat and let cool. In a small serving bowl, combine coconut, 1 cup **plain yogurt,** and 2 tablespoons **lemon juice.** If made ahead, cover and refrigerate for up to 2 hours. Makes about 1½ cups.

Per tablespoon: 21 calories, .59 g protein, 2 g carbohydrates, 1 g total fat, .56 mg cholesterol, 15 mg sodium

Baked Fish & Spinach Salad

Preparation time: About 20 minutes

Baking time: 5 to 10 minutes

Chilling time: At least 1 hour

Crisp spinach leaves encircle cold baked fish fillets crowned with a spicy curry dressing, sliced hard-cooked egg, and roasted cashews.

- 1½ **pounds skinless lean white-fleshed fish fillets, such as red (or other) snapper, rockfish, cod, or lingcod (½ to 1 inch thick)**
  Curry Dressing (recipe follows)
- ¾ **pound spinach, rinsed well**
- 1 **hard-cooked egg, thinly sliced**
- ¾ **cup roasted cashews, coarsely chopped**

Rinse fish and pat dry. Arrange in a single layer in a shallow baking pan. Bake, uncovered, in a 500° oven until fish is just slightly translucent or wet inside; cut in thickest part to test (5 to 10 minutes). Let cool in pan, then cover and refrigerate until chilled (at least 1 hour or up to 8 hours).

Prepare Curry Dressing and refrigerate. Pat spinach dry, remove stems, and tear into bite-size pieces if necessary. (At this point, you may wrap spinach in paper towels, enclose in a plastic bag, and refrigerate for up to 8 hours.)

Gently break fish into bite-size flakes; pull out and discard any small bones. Arrange spinach around rim of a large platter or individual plates. Mound fish in center. Spoon a little Curry Dressing over fish; garnish with sliced egg and roasted cashews. Pass remaining dressing to add to taste. Makes 4 servings.

Per serving: 325 calories, 37 g protein, 11 g carbohydrates, 15 g total fat, 157 mg cholesterol, 170 mg sodium

Curry Dressing. Combine ½ cup **sour cream** or plain yogurt, 2 teaspoons **Dijon mustard,** 1 teaspoon *each* **curry powder** and **white wine vinegar,** and ¼ teaspoon *each* **ground cumin** and **ground turmeric;** mix until well blended. If made ahead, cover and refrigerate for up to a day. Makes about ½ cup.

Per tablespoon: 34 calories, .48 g protein, .93 g carbohydrates, 3 g total fat, 6 mg cholesterol, 45 mg sodium

Microwave-poached Fish

Microwaving is an easy way to prepare moist, succulent fish steaks or fillets for salads and other cold dishes.

Rinse and pat dry 1 pound **fish steaks or fillets** (½ to ¾ inch thick). Arrange in an even layer in a greased 7- by 11-inch microwave-safe baking dish, positioning thickest parts toward outside of dish. If desired, season to taste with **melted butter** or margarine, paprika, fresh or dry herbs, or lemon juice. Cover with heavy-duty plastic wrap.

Microwave on **HIGH (100%)** for 3 to 5 minutes (depending on thickness of fish), giving dish a half turn after 2 minutes; then let stand, covered, for 3 minutes. The fish should be just slightly translucent or wet inside; cut in thickest part to test.

Fish in Fresh Herb Aspic with Horseradish Cream

Preparation time: About 45 minutes

Cooking time: About 40 minutes

Chilling time: At least 5 hours

Red-fleshed salmon combines with white fish in this cool molded salad. Offer a tangy sauce of horseradish and sour cream alongside.

- **Poaching Liquid (recipe on facing page)**
- 2 **pounds skinless white-fleshed fish fillets or steaks, such as halibut, rockfish, or cod (½ to 1 inch thick)**
- 1¼ **to 1½ pounds skinless salmon fillets or steaks (½ to 1 inch thick)**
- ½ **cup water**
- 2 **envelopes unflavored gelatin**
- ¾ **cup *each* thinly sliced green onions (including tops) and minced parsley**
  Salt
- 2 **whole green onions, split lengthwise**
  Horseradish Cream (recipe on facing page)

Prepare Poaching Liquid; reheat to boiling, if necessary. Rinse white-fleshed fish and salmon; drain. Arrange in Poaching Liquid, overlapping pieces so fish is submerged. Reduce heat, cover, and simmer until fish is just slightly translucent or wet inside; cut in thickest part to test (5 to 10 minutes). Lift fish from liquid with a slotted spatula, then cover and refrigerate.

Boil liquid rapidly over high heat, uncovered, until reduced to 3 cups (about 5 minutes). Pour through a fine wire strainer into a 1-quart measuring cup; discard residue. If necessary, add water to make 3 cups; set liquid aside.

In a 2-quart pan, combine the ½ cup water and gelatin; let stand for 5 minutes to soften. Place over medium heat and stir until gelatin is dissolved; blend in reduced Poaching Liquid. Refrigerate until mixture has the consistency of unbeaten egg whites (30 to 45 minutes). Stir in sliced onions and parsley; season to taste with salt. Remove any bones from fish; break fish into about 1-inch chunks.

Place halved onions in bottom of a 2½- to 3-quart ring mold. Spoon a ½-inch layer of gelatin mixture over onions. Distribute about a fourth of the fish chunks around the ring. Repeat layers of gelatin mixture and fish until all gelatin mixture and fish chunks are used. Press fish down firmly in gelatin mixture to make top as level as possible. Cover and refrigerate until firm (at least 4 hours or up to a day). Meanwhile, prepare Horseradish Cream; refrigerate.

To serve, dip mold to rim in hot tap water just until edges begin to liquefy (12 to 15 seconds). Carefully invert mold onto a platter; lift off mold. Return salad to refrigerator until firm (20 to 30 minutes). Cut into thick slices and offer Horseradish Cream to add to taste. Makes 8 to 10 servings.

Poaching Liquid. In a 4- to 5-quart pan, combine 1 quart **water,** ½ cup **dry white wine,** 6 *each* **whole allspice** and **whole black peppercorns,** 3 tablespoons **lemon juice,** and 1 large **onion,** sliced. Bring to a boil over high heat; then reduce heat, cover, and simmer for 20 minutes. If made ahead, cover and refrigerate for up to a day.

Per serving: 172 calories, 29 g protein, 2 g carbohydrates, 5 g total fat, 78 mg cholesterol, 82 mg sodium

Horseradish Cream. Stir together until blended 1½ cups **sour cream,** 1 tablespoon **lemon juice,** and 2 to 3 tablespoons **prepared horseradish.** If made ahead, cover and refrigerate for up to 2 days. Makes 1¾ cups.

Per tablespoon: 9 calories, .13 g protein, .30 g carbohydrates, .86 g total fat, 2 mg cholesterol, 3 mg sodium

Smoked Salmon & Watercress-Orange Salad

Preparation time: About 25 minutes

Baking time: 10 to 12 minutes

Succulent salmon fillet, smoked as it bakes, is served atop assorted greens and orange segments for an elegant entrée salad. Toasted pine nuts add a crunchy finishing touch.

- 3 **tablespoons liquid smoke**
- 1 **pound skinless salmon fillet, cut into ½-inch-wide strips**
- 2 **tablespoons pine nuts or slivered almonds**
- ¼ **cup seasoned rice wine vinegar (or ¼ cup white wine vinegar mixed with 2 to 3 teaspoons sugar and salt to taste)**
- ¼ **cup salad oil**
- 1 **teaspoon *each* Worcestershire and dry basil leaves**
- 2 **large oranges**
- 1 **quart *each* lightly packed watercress sprigs and bite-size pieces butter lettuce, washed and crisped**
  Salt

Pour liquid smoke into a deep 5- to 6-quart pan. Set a rack in pan. Arrange salmon in a single layer on rack and cover tightly. Bake in a 350° oven until salmon is just slightly translucent or wet inside; cut in thickest part to test (10 to 12 minutes).

Meanwhile, toast pine nuts in a small frying pan over medium heat until golden (3 to 5 minutes), shaking pan frequently. Let cool.

In a medium-size bowl, combine vinegar, oil, Worcestershire, and basil; stir with a whisk until well blended. With a sharp knife, cut peel and all white membrane from oranges. Holding oranges over the bowl of dressing to catch juice, cut between segments and lift them out.

In a large bowl, combine orange segments, watercress sprigs, butter lettuce, and dressing. Toss lightly to mix; season to taste with salt. Divide salad evenly among 4 dinner plates. Top each portion with salmon strips. Sprinkle with pine nuts. Makes 4 servings.

Per serving: 371 calories, 26 g protein, 16 g carbohydrates, 23 g total fat, 62 mg cholesterol, 83 mg sodium

Smoked Fish & Mushrooms with Chèvre Velvet

Preparation time: About 30 minutes

Catch of the day? It's your choice of smoked salmon, sablefish (black cod), or trout for this elegant luncheon salad. A smooth goat cheese dressing tops the fish.

> Chèvre Velvet (recipe follows)
> ½ **pound smoked salmon, sablefish (black cod), or trout**
> ½ **pound mushrooms, sliced**
> 2 **cups watercress sprigs, washed and crisped**
> 4 **hard-cooked eggs, thinly sliced**

Prepare Chèvre Velvet; set aside briefly.

Remove and discard skin and bones from fish, if necessary. If desired, thinly slice fish or separate it into flakes. Arrange fish and mushrooms on individual plates. Spoon Chèvre Velvet over salads; garnish with watercress sprigs and egg slices. Makes 4 salads.

Chèvre Velvet. Cut 4 to 5 ounces **soft ripened chèvre** with white rind (such as Bûcheron or chabis) into chunks; place in a blender or food processor with ½ cup **mayonnaise** and 1 **egg**. Whirl until smooth. Use at once.

Per serving: 481 calories, 25 g protein, 6 g carbohydrates, 40 g total fat, 398 mg cholesterol, 871 mg sodium

Chinese Fish & Bean Thread Salad

Preparation time: 25 to 30 minutes

Cooking time: About 10 minutes

Chilling time: At least 2 hours

An arresting blend of crisp textures and sweet-tart flavors gives this salad its appeal (look for the ingredients in Asian markets). As in Mexican seviche, the fresh raw fish is "cooked" in lemon juice for a few hours before serving.

> Salad oil
> 2 **ounces bean thread noodles**
> 3 **tablespoons sesame seeds**
> 1 **pound boneless and skinless tilefish or other deep-sea saltwater fish fillets (see page 6 for tips on using raw fish)**
> ¼ **cup lemon juice**
> Lemon-Honey Dressing (recipe follows)
> 2½ **quarts shredded iceberg lettuce (about a 1½-lb. head)**
> ½ cup *each* **thinly slivered green onions (including tops) and chopped fresh cilantro (coriander) leaves**
> ½ **cup pickled shallots, cut into thin slivers (optional)**
> ¼ **cup pickled ginger, cut into thin slivers**

In a heavy 3- to 4-quart pan, heat about 1 inch of oil to 375°F on a deep-frying thermometer. Tear bean threads apart into 4 to 6 small handfuls. Add a handful of bean threads to oil, pushing them down into oil and turning until all are puffy and crisp (about 30 seconds). Lift out with a wire strainer or slotted spoon and drain on paper towels. Repeat to cook remaining bean threads. Let cool. Meanwhile, toast sesame seeds in a small, heavy frying pan over low heat until golden (3 to 5 minutes), shaking pan frequently. Let cool. (At this point, you may store fried bean threads and toasted sesame seeds separately in airtight containers at room temperature for up to 2 days.)

Rinse fish, pat dry, and cut crosswise into ⅛-inch-wide slices. In a small bowl, mix fish and lemon juice. Cover and refrigerate, stirring occasionally, until fish is opaque throughout; cut to test (at least 2 hours or up to 12 hours). Drain off juice to use in Lemon-Honey Dressing; prepare dressing.

Place lettuce in a wide, shallow bowl. Top with fish, onions, cilantro, shallots (if used), ginger, sesame seeds, and bean threads. Pour on Lemon-Honey Dressing, mix lightly, and serve at once. Makes 6 servings.

Lemon-Honey Dressing. Stir together **lemon juice reserved from marinated fish**, 2 tablespoons *each* **soy sauce** and **salad oil**, 2 to 3 tablespoons **honey**, 1 tablespoon **Dijon mustard**, 1 tablespoon **Oriental sesame oil** or salad oil, ¾ teaspoon grated **lemon peel**, and 1 clove **garlic**, minced or pressed.

Per serving: 257 calories, 17 g protein, 24 g carbohydrates, 11 g total fat, 26 mg cholesterol, 550 mg sodium

Delicate seafood contrasts with crisp, juicy fruit in simple Shrimp & Asian Pear Salad (recipe on page 48). To play up the mild flavors of shrimp and pears, drizzle each serving with a nippy mustard dressing.

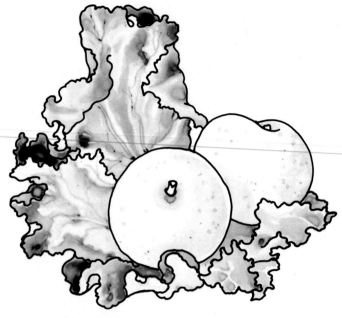

Skewered Shrimp with Papaya-Avocado Salad

Preparation time: 30 to 35 minutes

Chilling & soaking time: About 30 minutes

Cooking time: 6 to 8 minutes

A tart vinaigrette speckled with papaya seeds makes a good marinade for plump shrimp—and a tasty dressing for the crisp romaine lettuce served with them.

- 1 **medium-size ripe papaya**
  Papaya-Lime Dressing (recipe follows)
- 16 **extra-jumbo raw shrimp (16 to 20 per lb.), shelled and deveined**
- 2 **quarts lightly packed bite-size pieces romaine lettuce, washed and crisped**
- 3 **green onions (including tops), thinly sliced**
- 1 **large avocado**
- ⅓ **cup chopped macadamia nuts**
  Lime wedges

Peel and halve papaya; scoop out seeds, reserving 1 tablespoon for Papaya-Lime Dressing (discard remaining seeds). Thinly slice papaya and set aside. Prepare Papaya-Lime Dressing.

Place shrimp in a shallow baking dish; pour dressing over shrimp, cover, and refrigerate for about 30 minutes. Also soak 8 thin bamboo skewers in water to cover for 30 minutes.

Meanwhile, in a large bowl, combine lettuce, onions, and papaya; cover and refrigerate until ready to grill shrimp.

Lift shrimp from dressing; reserve dressing. Thread shrimp on 4 pairs of skewers, aligning skewers parallel so shrimp lie flat; set aside. Halve and pit avocado; using a melon ball cutter, scoop avocado into ¾-inch-diameter balls. Add to dressing, mixing lightly to coat.

Place skewered shrimp on a greased grill 4 to 6 inches above a solid bed of hot coals. Cook, turning once, until shrimp are opaque throughout; cut to test (6 to 8 minutes *total*).

Add avocado balls and dressing to lettuce mixture; lift with 2 spoons to mix lightly. Divide salad among 4 dinner plates; add a skewer of hot grilled shrimp to each. Sprinkle with macadamia nuts and garnish with lime wedges. Makes 4 servings.

Papaya-Lime Dressing. In a blender or food processor, combine ⅓ cup **salad oil**, ¼ cup **olive oil**, 2 tablespoons **tarragon wine vinegar**, 1 tablespoon

Pictured on page 47

Shrimp & Asian Pear Salad

Preparation time: 15 to 20 minutes

Juicy Asian pears, also called apple pears, offer a crisp contrast to the succulent shrimp and leafy greens in this quick salad. Serve it for lunch or a light supper.

- **Mustard Dressing (recipe follows)**
- 4 **to 8 large romaine lettuce leaves, washed and crisped**
- 4 **to 8 red oak-leaf or small red leaf lettuce leaves, washed and crisped**
- 4 **medium-size Asian pears (6 to 8 oz. *each*), thinly sliced crosswise**
- 1 **pound tiny cooked and shelled shrimp**
  Fresh tarragon sprigs (optional)
  Salt and freshly ground pepper

Prepare Mustard Dressing. Arrange romaine and oak-leaf lettuce on individual dinner plates; add pears and shrimp, dividing them evenly among plates. Drizzle dressing over shrimp and fruit. Garnish with tarragon sprigs, if desired. Season to taste with salt and pepper. Makes 4 servings.

Mustard Dressing. Combine ½ cup **olive oil,** ¼ cup **white wine vinegar,** 1 tablespoon **Dijon mustard,** and 1 tablespoon minced **fresh tarragon leaves** or ½ teaspoon dry tarragon. Mix until well blended.

Per serving: 454 calories, 25 g protein, 25 g carbohydrates, 29 g total fat, 221 mg cholesterol, 369 mg sodium

lime juice, ¼ teaspoon **salt,** and 1 teaspoon **Dijon mustard;** whirl until well combined. Add reserved 1 tablespoon **papaya seeds** and ½ teaspoon grated **lime peel;** whirl until seeds are the consistency of coarsely ground pepper.

Per serving: 611 calories, 24 g protein, 19 g carbohydrates, 51 g total fat, 140 mg cholesterol, 329 mg sodium

Shrimp Slaw with Cucumber Dressing

Preparation time: About 20 minutes

If you're looking for a light and colorful main-dish salad, try this dressed-up version of an old favorite. Diced red bell pepper, a refreshing cucumber dressing, and plenty of tiny shrimp give familiar coleslaw a whole new look.

- 1 **small head cabbage (about 1¼ lbs.)**
- 1 **medium-size red bell pepper, seeded and diced**
- 4 **green onions (including tops), thinly sliced**
- 12 **pimento-stuffed olives, thinly sliced**
- 1 **pound tiny cooked and shelled shrimp**
- ¼ **teaspoon *each* caraway seeds, celery seeds, and dill weed**
  Cucumber Dressing (recipe follows)
  Salt and pepper
  Chopped chives (optional)

Finely shred cabbage; you should have 8 to 9 cups, lightly packed. In a large bowl, combine cabbage, bell pepper, onions, olives, shrimp, caraway seeds, celery seeds, and dill; mix lightly. (At this point, you may cover and refrigerate for up to 8 hours.)

Prepare Cucumber Dressing. Add dressing to cabbage mixture; mix gently. Season to taste with salt and pepper. Garnish with chives, if desired. Makes 6 servings.

Cucumber Dressing. Stir together until smoothly blended 1 cup *each* **mayonnaise** and peeled, seeded, finely chopped **cucumber;** 1 tablespoon chopped **chives;** 2 tablespoons **rice wine vinegar;** 3 tablespoons chopped **parsley;** and ½ teaspoon grated **lemon peel.**

Per serving: 380 calories, 18 g protein, 9 g carbohydrates, 31 g total fat, 169 mg cholesterol, 567 mg sodium

Shrimp, Endive & Avocado Salad

Preparation time: About 10 minutes

Cooking time: About 10 minutes

Bold curry seasonings lend assertive flavor to a saucy dip for shrimp, sliced avocado, and Belgian endive spears. Use extra-jumbo shrimp, steeped as directed on page 51; or substitute cooked, shelled tiny shrimp.

- ¾ **cup mayonnaise**
- 2 **teaspoons mustard seeds**
- ¼ **teaspoon *each* ground cumin and curry powder**
- 1 **large avocado**
- 12 **to 15 extra-jumbo cooked shrimp in shells (16 to 20 per lb.) or ¾ pound tiny cooked and shelled shrimp**
- 1 **large head Belgian endive, separated into leaves (or 12 to 15 small inner romaine lettuce leaves), washed and crisped**

Stir together mayonnaise, mustard seeds, cumin, and curry powder. Spoon a third of the mayonnaise mixture into center of each of 3 dinner plates (or divide it among 3 small bowls; place each on a plate).

Pit, peel, and slice avocado. Divide avocado slices, shrimp, and endive equally among plates. To eat, shell shrimp and dip them into mayonnaise mixture along with avocado and endive. (If using tiny cooked and shelled shrimp, eat with forks, dipping each bite into mayonnaise mixture.) Makes 3 servings.

Per serving: 657 calories, 27 g protein, 9 g carbohydrates, 58 g total fat, 254 mg cholesterol, 577 mg sodium

A shower of toasted black sesame seeds adds sophisticated interest to Crab Salad with Cucumber & Radishes
(recipe on page 52). If you like, spoon the salad over
romaine leaves and garnish with whole radishes.

Mustard Shrimp with Chilled Lemon Noodles

Preparation time: About 30 minutes

Chilling time: At least 1 hour

Cooking time: 15 to 20 minutes

Need a handsome summertime entrée? Spoon cold mustard-flavored shrimp over lemony buckwheat noodles and crisp watercress.

    3 tablespoons salad oil
    3 cloves garlic, minced or pressed
   ⅓ cup thinly sliced green onions (including tops)
   ⅛ teaspoon ground red pepper (cayenne)
  1½ pounds medium-large raw shrimp (30 to 35 per lb.), shelled and deveined
    3 tablespoons *each* dry sherry and white wine vinegar
    1 tablespoon Dijon mustard
    1 tablespoon finely chopped fresh tarragon leaves or 1 teaspoon dry tarragon
       Lemon Dressing (recipe follows)
   12 ounces dry thin Japanese-style buckwheat noodles (*soba*) or vermicelli
    2 quarts watercress sprigs or mixed small lettuce leaves, washed and crisped

Heat oil in a wide frying pan over medium heat. Add garlic, onions, and red pepper; cook, stirring often, until onions are limp (2 to 3 minutes). Add shrimp and cook, stirring, until opaque throughout; cut to test (4 to 5 minutes). Add sherry, vinegar, mustard, and tarragon; bring to a boil, stirring. Remove from heat and let cool; then cover and refrigerate for at least 1 hour or up to 8 hours. Prepare Lemon Dressing and set aside.

In a 5- to 6-quart pan, cook noodles in 4 quarts of boiling water just until tender to bite (about 10 minutes); or cook according to package directions. Drain noodles; rinse with cold water until cool, then drain again. Mix noodles lightly with Lemon Dressing. (At this point, you may cover and refrigerate for up to 8 hours.)

Arrange watercress on a platter. Spoon noodle mixture over watercress; top with shrimp mixture. Makes 4 to 6 servings.

Lemon Dressing. Stir together ⅓ cup **lemon juice**, 3 tablespoons **soy sauce**, 1 tablespoon *each* **Oriental sesame oil** and finely chopped **fresh ginger**, and 2 teaspoons **sugar.**

Per serving: 418 calories, 28 g protein, 50 g carbohydrates, 12 g total fat, 140 mg cholesterol, 750 mg sodium

Shrimp & Litchi Salad

Preparation time: About 20 minutes

Cooking time: 6 to 8 minutes

Sweet canned litchis (or related fruits such as longans or rambutans) bring exotic flavor to this refreshing salad of steeped shrimp, watercress sprigs, and sliced cucumber. You'll find the fruit in Asian markets and some well-stocked supermarkets.

    1 pound medium-large shrimp (30 to 35 per lb.), shelled (except for tails) and deveined
    1 can (20 oz.) litchis, longans, or rambutans packed in syrup
   ¼ cup salad oil
    2 tablespoons lemon juice
    2 cups sliced European or English cucumber
    1 quart lightly packed watercress sprigs, washed and crisped
       Salt and freshly ground pepper

Rinse shrimp. Steep as directed below. Meanwhile, drain litchis, reserving 2 tablespoons of the syrup (discard remaining syrup or reserve for other uses). In a large bowl, combine oil, reserved 2 tablespoons syrup, and lemon juice; mix well. If desired, cut fruit pieces in half; add to dressing along with drained shrimp, cucumber, and watercress. Mix lightly. Divide salad evenly among 4 dinner plates; season to taste with salt and pepper. Makes 4 servings.

Per serving: 331 calories, 20 g protein, 30 g carbohydrates, 16 g total fat, 140 mg cholesterol, 201 mg sodium

Steeped Shrimp for Salads

Steeping is an extra-gentle cooking method that's beautifully suited to shrimp—they retain all their natural succulence. If you wish, remove the sand vein neatly with a skewer (see page 73) before steeping the shellfish.

In a 3- to 4-quart pan, bring 1 quart **water** to a boil over high heat. Remove pan from heat and quickly add 1 pound **raw shrimp in shells.** Cover tightly and let stand until shrimp are opaque throughout; cut to test (6 to 8 minutes). Drain, cool quickly in cold water, and drain again.

Celery Root & Shellfish Salad

Preparation time: *About 20 minutes*

Cooking time: *5 to 8 minutes*

Chilling time: *At least 1¼ hours*

Crisp celery root contrasts deliciously with tender shellfish in this stylish salad plate. For each serving, spoon scallops, shrimp, and crab in a creamy dressing alongside a simple celery root vinaigrette; garnish with endive spears and thin lemon wedges.

> **Celery Root Vinaigrette (recipe follows)**
> ½ **pound sea scallops**
> ½ **cup whipping cream**
> 1½ **teaspoons lemon juice**
> ¾ **teaspoon dry tarragon**
> ¼ **pound** *each* **cooked crabmeat and tiny cooked and shelled shrimp**
> **Salt**
> 2 **tablespoons finely chopped watercress or parsley**
> 12 **Belgian endive leaves or small inner romaine lettuce leaves, washed and crisped**
> 12 **thin lemon wedges**
> **Watercress or parsley sprigs**
> **Freshly ground pepper**

Prepare Celery Root Vinaigrette and refrigerate.

Rinse scallops, pat dry, and cut into bite-size pieces. Set aside. In a 1½- to 2-quart pan, combine cream, lemon juice, and tarragon. Bring to a boil over high heat. Add scallops, reduce heat, and simmer, uncovered, until scallops are opaque throughout; cut to test (about 1½ minutes). With a slotted spoon, transfer scallops to a bowl; cover and refrigerate. Increase heat to high and boil cream mixture until reduced to ⅓ cup (about 1½ minutes); cover and refrigerate until cold (at least 15 minutes).

To scallops, add chilled cream mixture, crab, and shrimp; season to taste with salt. (At this point, you may cover and refrigerate for up to 8 hours.) Stir in chopped watercress.

For each serving, place a mound of Celery Root Vinaigrette and a mound of seafood mixture on a dinner plate. Alongside, place 3 endive spears and 3 lemon wedges. Garnish with watercress sprigs and pepper. Makes 4 servings.

Celery Root Vinaigrette. In a 3- to 4-quart pan, combine 2 cups **water** and ½ cup **distilled white vinegar;** bring to a boil over high heat. Meanwhile, scrub ¾ pound **celery root** well; then peel, cut into matchstick pieces, and immediately add to vinegar mixture. Return to a boil and cook, uncovered, until celery root is tender-crisp to bite (about 30 seconds); drain well.

In a bowl, combine celery root, 2 tablespoons **salad oil,** and 1 tablespoon minced **shallot** or red onion; season to taste with **salt.** Cover and refrigerate for at least 1 hour or up to 8 hours. Just before serving, mix in 2 tablespoons finely chopped **watercress** or parsley.

Per serving: 371 calories, 24 g protein, 13 g carbohydrates, 26 g total fat, 165 mg cholesterol, 330 mg sodium

Pictured on page 50

Crab Salad with Cucumber & Radishes

Preparation time: *About 15 minutes*

In a delicate interplay of flavors and textures, tender crabmeat and crisp, crunchy cucumbers and radishes are all tossed together in tangy rice wine vinegar. A sprinkling of black sesame seeds (available in Asian markets) adds distinction.

> 1 **teaspoon black sesame seeds (optional)**
> 1 **large European or English cucumber (about 1½ lbs.)**
> 1 **green onion (including top), thinly sliced**
> 10 **medium-size radishes, thinly sliced**
> ½ **to 1 pound cooked crabmeat**
> ⅓ **to ½ cup seasoned rice wine vinegar (or ⅓ to ½ cup white wine vinegar mixed with 4 teaspoons sugar)**
> **Salt**
> **Romaine lettuce leaves, washed and crisped**
> **Slivered green onion tops (optional)**
> **Whole radishes (optional)**

If using sesame seeds, toast them in a small, heavy frying pan over low heat until they become fragrant (3 to 5 minutes), shaking pan frequently. Set aside.

Cut cucumber lengthwise into quarters; thinly slice crosswise. In a large bowl, lightly mix cucumber, sliced onion, sliced radishes, crab, and vinegar; season to taste with salt. Spoon mixture over lettuce leaves. Sprinkle with sesame seeds (if used); if desired, garnish with slivered onion tops and whole radishes. Makes 4 servings.

Per serving: 102 calories, 12 g protein, 10 g carbohydrates, 1 g total fat, 57 mg cholesterol, 165 mg sodium

Crab Chat

Preparation time: About 20 minutes

Cooking time: About 10 minutes

Cooling time: At least 30 minutes

In India, *chat* means more than small talk. It's a boldly seasoned snack, appetizer, or—in this case—a salad to excite the palate.

- 2 tablespoons salad oil
- 1 small onion, finely chopped
- 1 tablespoon minced fresh ginger
- 2 cloves garlic, minced or pressed
- 2 teaspoons paprika
- ½ teaspoon *each* ground red pepper (cayenne) and dry thyme leaves
- 1 teaspoon fennel seeds, crushed
- 5 medium-size pear-shaped (Roma-type) tomatoes (about 1 lb. *total*), chopped
- 1 pound cooked crabmeat
- 3 tablespoons lemon juice
- ⅓ cup chopped fresh cilantro (coriander)
  Salt
  Iceberg lettuce leaves, washed and crisped
- 2 green onions (including tops), thinly sliced
  Lemon wedges

Heat oil in a wide frying pan over medium heat. Add chopped onion, ginger, and garlic. Cook, stirring often, until onion is limp (4 to 5 minutes). Stir in paprika, red pepper, thyme, fennel seeds, and half the tomatoes. Cook, uncovered, stirring occasionally, until sauce is reduced to a thick pulp (about 5 minutes). Remove from heat and stir in

crab and lemon juice. Let cool (at least 30 minutes) or cover and refrigerate for up to 8 hours.

Stir in cilantro and about 1 cup of the remaining tomatoes; season to taste with salt. Line a platter with lettuce; spoon crab mixture on top. Garnish with remaining tomatoes and green onions. Serve with lemon wedges to squeeze over each serving to taste. Makes 5 or 6 servings.

Per serving: 143 calories, 16 g protein, 6 g carbohydrates, 6 g total fat, 76 mg cholesterol, 220 mg sodium

Cracked Crab & Yellow Rice Salad

Preparation time: About 30 minutes

Cooking time: 3 to 5 minutes

Build a handsome seafood feast for two with cracked crab, tender-crisp asparagus, and turmeric-tinted rice.

Turmeric Dressing (recipe follows)
- 1 cooked large Dungeness crab (about 2½ lbs.), cleaned and cracked (save uncracked back shell); or ½ to ¾ pound cooked crabmeat
- 1 pound asparagus, tough ends removed
- 1½ cups cold cooked long-grain white rice
- ⅓ cup thinly sliced green onions (including tops)
  Salt and pepper
  Chopped parsley

Prepare Turmeric Dressing and set aside.

Rinse crab back shell; set aside. Remove meat from body of crab; discard shells. Mound crabmeat on one side of a large platter; arrange unshelled legs and claws around meat. Top with reserved back shell; refrigerate.

In a wide frying pan, bring 1 inch of water to a boil over high heat. Add asparagus and cook, uncovered, just until tender-crisp to bite (2 to 4 minutes). Drain, immerse in cold water until cool, and drain again. Arrange on platter with crab. Spoon about a third of Turmeric Dressing over asparagus.

Mix remaining Turmeric Dressing with rice and onions; season to taste with salt and pepper. Mound rice mixture on platter; garnish with parsley. Makes 2 servings.

Turmeric Dressing. Combine ⅓ cup **salad oil,** 2 tablespoons **white wine vinegar,** 2 teaspoons **Dijon mustard,** and ½ teaspoon **ground turmeric;** whisk until well blended.

Per serving: 593 calories, 29 g protein, 33 g carbohydrates, 39 g total fat, 114 mg cholesterol, 470 mg sodium

Calamari Salad al Pesto

Preparation time: About 25 minutes

Cooking time: 5 to 7 minutes

Chilling time: At least 3 hours

Convenient giant squid steaks—cleaned, pounded, and ready to use upon purchase—play the starring role in this hearty main-dish salad. Cut the steaks into strips, then stir-fry and toss with pesto and crisp vegetables.

- ¼ cup olive oil
- 1 small onion, finely chopped
- 2 cloves garlic, minced or pressed
- 3 tablespoons chopped walnuts
- 1 pound tenderized giant squid (calamari) steaks, cut into ¼-inch-wide strips
- 2 tablespoons dry sherry
  Pesto Sauce (recipe follows)
- 1 medium-size red bell pepper, seeded and finely chopped
- ¼ cup finely chopped celery
- 2 tablespoons finely chopped parsley
- ¼ cup cider vinegar
- 1 tablespoon lemon juice
  Salt and pepper
  About 1 quart shredded iceberg lettuce

Heat oil in a wide frying pan over medium heat. Add onion, garlic, and walnuts. Cook, stirring often, until onion is soft and nuts are toasted (about 5 minutes). Add squid and sherry and cook, stirring constantly, just until squid looks opaque (about 1 minute; do not overcook). With a slotted spoon, transfer squid mixture to a large bowl and set aside. Discard cooking juices.

Prepare Pesto Sauce; add to squid mixture along with bell pepper, celery, parsley, vinegar, and lemon juice. Mix lightly. Season to taste with salt and pepper. Cover and refrigerate for at least 3 hours or for up to a day.

Line a serving bowl or deep platter with shredded lettuce. Spoon squid mixture over lettuce. Makes 6 servings.

Pesto Sauce. In a blender or food processor, combine ¼ cup **olive oil,** ⅓ cup lightly packed **fresh basil leaves,** 2 tablespoons **pine nuts,** and 1 clove **garlic** (thinly sliced); whirl until puréed.

Per serving: 291 calories, 14 g protein, 9 g carbohydrates, 23 g total fat, 176 mg cholesterol, 44 mg sodium

Pictured on facing page

Warm Green Salad with Mussels

Preparation time: About 20 minutes

Cooking time: 35 to 40 minutes

Wilted slightly by the warmth of a creamy wine sauce, shredded mustard greens impart a pleasantly pungent flavor to this first-course salad.

- 1½ pounds mussels in shells
- 1½ cups dry white wine
- 1 bottle (8 oz.) clam juice
- 1 medium-size carrot, minced
- 1 small onion, minced
- ½ cup whipping cream
- 1 small head butter lettuce, separated into leaves, washed and crisped
- 1 quart finely shredded mustard greens

Prepare mussels (see page 13). In a 5- to 6-quart pan, combine mussels and wine. Cover tightly, bring to a boil over medium-high heat, and boil gently until mussels open (about 5 minutes). Uncover and let stand until cool enough to handle. Remove mussels from pan, reserving cooking liquid; discard any unopened mussels. Then remove remaining mussels from shells; discard shells. Set mussels aside.

Pour cooking liquid through a fine wire strainer into a wide frying pan. Add clam juice, carrot, and onion. Bring to a boil over high heat; boil, uncovered, until reduced by half (12 to 15 minutes). Stir in cream. Continue to boil, stirring often, until reduced to about 1 cup (12 to 15 minutes). Gently stir in mussels and keep warm over lowest heat.

Divide lettuce among 4 plates; on each plate, group leaves to form a cup. Mound a fourth of the mustard greens in center of each lettuce cup. Spoon mussels and sauce onto mustard greens. Serve at once. Makes 4 servings.

Per serving: 164 calories, 9 g protein, 9 g carbohydrates, 11 g total fat, 47 mg cholesterol, 308 mg sodium

An elegant first course for a chilly autumn evening,
Warm Green Salad with Mussels (recipe on facing page)
mingles the tender, tawny shellfish with shredded
mustard greens wilted by the heat of the dressing.

Add sizzle to a cool salad with seafood hot off the grill. Accompanied with chilled white wine and a loaf of crusty bread, any of these hot-and-cold combinations makes a light but satisfying repast.

Fresh Tuna & Wild Rice Salad

- 3 **tablespoons olive oil**
- 1 **tablespoon** *each* **red wine vinegar and tarragon-flavored Dijon mustard**
- 1 **clove garlic, minced or pressed**
- 1 to 1½ **pounds boneless and skinless fresh tuna, such as albacore, bluefin, or yellowfin (¾ to 1 inch thick)**
- ⅔ **cup wild rice, rinsed and drained**
- 1¾ **cups water**
- ½ **cup** *each* **sliced pimento-stuffed olives and sliced celery**
- 2 **hard-cooked eggs, chopped**
- 2 **green onions (including tops), thinly sliced**
- 2 **tablespoons chopped parsley**
- 1 **tablespoon lemon juice**
- ⅓ **cup mayonnaise**
  Salt and pepper
  Butter lettuce leaves, washed and crisped

In a shallow 2-quart baking dish, combine oil, vinegar, mustard, and garlic; mix well. Rinse tuna and pat dry. Add to oil mixture; turn to coat well on both sides. Cover and refrigerate while preparing rice (or for up to a day).

In a 1- to 1½-quart pan, combine rice and water. Bring to a boil over high heat; reduce heat, cover, and simmer until rice is tender to bite (about 25 minutes). Drain well and fluff with a fork. Let cool, then place in a large bowl and add olives, celery, eggs, onions, parsley, lemon juice, and mayonnaise. Mix lightly; season to taste with salt and pepper. (At this point, you may cover and refrigerate for up to a day.)

Grilled Seafood Salads

Place tuna on a greased grill about 6 inches above a solid bed of hot coals. Cook, turning once, until just slightly translucent or wet inside; cut in thickest part to test (3 to 4 minutes *total*).

To serve, line individual plates with lettuce, then top with rice salad. Cut hot grilled tuna into ½-inch-wide strips and place alongside rice salad. Makes 4 servings.

Per serving: 549 calories, 34 g protein, 23 g carbohydrates, 35 g total fat, 191 mg cholesterol, 719 mg sodium

Grilled Salmon Swirls with Chèvre Toasts

- 2 **tablespoons butter or margarine**
- 1 **tablespoon** *each* **Dijon mustard and dry sherry**
- 2 **pieces tail-end salmon fillet (1 to 1¼ lbs.** *total***), skinned**
  Chèvre Toasts (recipe follows)
- 2 **tablespoons red wine vinegar**
- 1 **small shallot, finely chopped**
- ⅓ **cup olive oil**
  Salt and pepper
- 2 **quarts lightly packed bite-size pieces red or green butter lettuce, washed and crisped**

Melt butter in a small pan over medium-low heat. Stir in mustard and sherry; remove from heat.

Place salmon fillets on a flat surface, skinned sides down. Brush with some of the butter mixture (reserve remaining butter mixture). Starting at a narrow end, roll up each fillet pinwheel fashion. Cut each roll crosswise into slices about 1 inch thick. Divide "pinwheels" among 4 skewers, piercing pinwheels horizontally to secure them on skewers. Cover and refrigerate while preparing Chèvre Toasts.

While Chèvre Toasts are baking, blend vinegar, shallot, and oil; season to taste with salt and pepper. Set dressing aside.

Place salmon skewers on a well-greased grill 4 to 6 inches above a solid bed of medium coals. Brush with some of the remaining butter mixture. Cook, turning once with a wide spatula and brushing again with remaining butter mixture, until salmon is just slightly translucent or wet inside; cut in thickest part to test (8 to 10 minutes *total*).

Stir dressing to blend. Mix dressing lightly with lettuce; arrange on individual plates. Top each plate with a salmon skewer and garnish with hot Chèvre Toasts. Makes 4 servings.

Chèvre Toasts. Blend 3 ounces **soft fresh or ripened goat cheese,** 1 tablespoon *each* **olive oil** and chopped **chives,** and ⅛ teaspoon coarsely ground **pepper.** Spread over 8 to 12 thin **French bread baguette** slices. Arrange bread slices on a baking sheet, cheese side up. Bake in a 350° oven until edges of bread are golden brown (10 to 12 minutes).

Per serving: 595 calories, 31 g protein, 24 g carbohydrates, 42 g total fat, 99 mg cholesterol, 538 mg sodium

Mussels Vinaigrette

Preparation time: About 30 minutes

Cooking time: About 8 minutes

Mussels steamed in wine join red-skinned potatoes, peas, and tomatoes in a colorful salad. For a Mediterranean-style supper, serve with hot garlic bread and fruity red wine.

 5 **pounds mussels in shells**
 1 **teaspoon dry thyme leaves**
 ½ **cup plus 2 tablespoons olive oil**
 ½ **cup dry white wine**
 ¾ **pound small red thin-skinned potatoes (*each* about 1½ inches in diameter), cooked and quartered**
 1½ **pounds firm-ripe tomatoes, cut into 1-inch chunks**
 1 **small onion, thinly sliced**
 ½ **cup frozen peas, thawed**
 ⅓ **cup *each* distilled white vinegar and finely chopped parsley**
 Salt

Prepare mussels (see page 13).

In a 5- to 6-quart pan, combine thyme and 2 tablespoons *each* of the oil and wine. Add mussels. Cover tightly, bring to a boil over medium-high heat, and cook until shells open (about 8 minutes). Uncover and let stand until cool enough to handle. Discard liquid and any unopened mussels.

Remove mussels from shells; discard shells. In a large, shallow serving bowl, lightly mix mussels, potatoes, tomatoes, onion, peas, vinegar, parsley, remaining ½ cup oil, and remaining 6 tablespoons wine. Season to taste with salt. If made ahead, cover and refrigerate for up to 4 hours; serve at room temperature. Makes 6 servings.

Per serving: 379 calories, 16 g protein, 24 g carbohydrates, 25 g total fat, 31 mg cholesterol, 342 mg sodium

Fennel Salad with Clams

Preparation time: About 25 minutes

Cooking time: About 20 minutes

Cooling & chilling time: About 30 minutes

With its celerylike texture and mild licorice flavor, fresh fennel provides an exquisite foil for steamed clams in a tart wine sauce.

 4 **green onions (including tops)**
 1 **cup *each* dry white wine and water**
 ½ **teaspoon fennel seeds**
 24 **small hard-shell clams in shells, suitable for steaming, scrubbed**
 3 **tablespoons lemon juice**
 2 **large heads fennel (1½ to 2 lbs. *total*)**
 Lemon wedges

Thinly slice white part of onions; reserve green tops for garnish. In a 5- to 6-quart pan, combine sliced onions, wine, water, and fennel seeds. Cover and bring to a boil over high heat. Add clams; reduce heat, cover, and boil gently until clams open (5 to 10 minutes). Lift out clams, returning any juices to pan; discard any unopened clams. Let remaining clams stand until cool enough to handle, then remove from shells; discard shells.

Strain cooking liquid, then bring to a boil over high heat; boil, uncovered, until reduced to ⅓ cup (10 to 12 minutes). Let cool slightly, then stir in lemon juice.

Trim and discard bases of fennel heads. Remove and reserve leaves. Cut out any bruised areas, then cut each head lengthwise into quarters; remove and discard core and tough stems. Thinly slice crosswise (you should have about 4 cups).

In a bowl, combine fennel, clams, and reduced cooking liquid. Cover and refrigerate for about 15 minutes. Arrange reserved onion tops across 4 dinner plates; mound salad over onion tops on each. Garnish with lemon wedges and reserved fennel leaves. Makes 4 servings.

Per serving: 94 calories, 13 g protein, 8 g carbohydrates, 1 g total fat, 31 mg cholesterol, 165 mg sodium

Pop the cork on a bottle of bubbly for this elegant dinner for two—tempting Spinach Pasta & Salmon in Champagne Cream Sauce (recipe on facing page).

Pasta & Rice

Generations of shellfish lovers have savored seafood with pasta or rice: linguine with clam sauce and curried shrimp over rice are two classic combinations. In this chapter, we present some new candidates for stardom.

Among pasta first courses, elegant possibilities include Red & Black Lemon Pasta and Salmon Ravioli with Basil Sauce. For the main event, you'll want to try Spinach Pasta & Salmon in Champagne Cream Sauce, Risotto & Shrimp Primavera, and many more. It won't be long before you're revising your list of favorites!

Pictured on facing page

Spinach Pasta & Salmon in Champagne Cream Sauce

Preparation time: About 5 minutes

Cooking time: About 20 minutes

Accompany this sophisticated pasta entrée with more of the same champagne used to poach the salmon.

- 1 **cup brut champagne**
- 2 **cups water**
- ½ **teaspoon whole allspice**
- 1 **bay leaf**
- ½ **pound salmon fillet (¾ to 1 inch thick)**
- 1¼ **cups whipping cream**
- 6 **ounces dry spinach egg noodles**
- 2 **tablespoons butter or margarine**
  Salt and pepper
- ¼ **cup 2-inch-long chive strips; or ¼ cup thinly sliced green onions (including tops)**

In a wide frying pan, combine champagne, water, allspice, and bay leaf. Bring to a boil over high heat. Add salmon, reduce heat, cover, and simmer until just slightly translucent or wet inside; cut in thickest part to test (5 to 10 minutes). Lift out fish, reserving poaching liquid. Carefully remove and discard skin and any bones from fish, then break flesh into bite-size pieces; set aside.

Pour poaching liquid through a fine wire strainer into a bowl; discard seasonings. Return liquid to frying pan and add cream. Bring to a boil over high heat; boil, uncovered, stirring occasionally, until reduced to 1¼ cups. Keep warm over lowest heat.

While you are reducing cream mixture, in a 4- to 5-quart pan, cook noodles in 3 quarts of boiling water just until tender to bite (5 to 7 minutes); or cook according to package directions. Drain noodles; add noodles and butter to cream mixture. Season to taste with salt and pepper, then add salmon. Mix lightly, using 2 forks. Serve sprinkled with chives. Makes 4 first-course or 2 main-dish servings.

Per first-course serving: 519 calories, 19 g protein, 33 g carbohydrates, 35 g total fat, 170 mg cholesterol, 114 mg sodium

Salmon Ravioli with Basil Sauce

Preparation time: About 45 minutes

Cooking time: 20 to 25 minutes

Though sauced with a favorite Italian herb, these oversized ravioli bear little resemblance to Italy's familiar meat- or cheese-stuffed dumplings. Made with purchased egg roll skins, they're filled with a fluffy fish mousse much like that used for French *quenelles*. If you like, use scallops instead of salmon in the filling; the result will be equally exquisite.

      Salmon Mousse (recipe follows)
12 egg roll or spring roll skins (noodle type)
 1 egg, beaten
      Basil Sauce (recipe follows)
 1 tablespoon butter or margarine
 1 clove garlic, minced or pressed
 1 small tomato, peeled and diced
      Salt and pepper
      Fresh basil sprigs

Prepare Salmon Mousse. For each ravioli, place one-twelfth of the Salmon Mousse in center of an egg roll skin (keep remaining skins covered with plastic wrap). Brush skin around half the filling with egg. Fold plain side of skin over filling, aligning edges; press firmly to seal. Trim edges with a pastry wheel, cutting rectangle into a semicircle (folded edge should be 4 inches long). Discard egg roll skin trimmings.

Place filled ravioli in a single layer, edges not touching, on rimmed baking sheets. (At this point, you may cover with plastic wrap and refrigerate for up to 4 hours. Or freeze until solid, then package in freezer bags and freeze for up to 2 months. Do not thaw frozen ravioli before cooking.)

Prepare Basil Sauce.

Melt butter in a small frying pan over medium heat. Add garlic; cook, stirring, until golden. Add tomato and cook, stirring, until almost all juices have evaporated. Season to taste with salt and pepper. (At this point, you may cover and let stand for up to 6 hours; reheat to serve.)

In a 5- to 6-quart pan, cook ravioli in 4 quarts of boiling water just until pasta is an even color throughout and is tender to bite (about 5 minutes; 6 to 7 minutes if frozen).

To serve, spoon Basil Sauce onto 6 large plates. Remove ravioli from heat; using a slotted spoon, lift from water, draining well. Arrange 2 ravioli atop sauce on each plate. Garnish each serving with sautéed tomato mixture and basil sprigs. Makes 6 first-course servings.

Salmon Mousse. Rinse and pat dry ½ pound **salmon fillet** or steak. Remove and discard skin and any bones; cut flesh into chunks. In a food processor or blender, combine salmon, 1 **egg white,** ⅓ cup **whipping cream,** and 2 teaspoons chopped **chives;** whirl until smoothly puréed. Season to taste with **salt** and **ground white pepper.** If made ahead, cover and refrigerate for up to 24 hours.

Basil Sauce. Melt 2 tablespoons **butter** or margarine in a wide frying pan over medium-high heat. Add 2 teaspoons minced **shallot** and cook, stirring, until soft (2 to 3 minutes). Stir in 3 tablespoons **dry white wine,** 1 tablespoon **dry sherry,** and ½ cup *each* **regular-strength chicken broth** and chopped **mushrooms.** Cook, uncovered, stirring occasionally, until reduced to ½ cup; remove from heat.

In a food processor or blender, combine hot mushroom mixture and 3 cups lightly packed **fresh basil leaves;** whirl until smooth. Return mixture to pan. (At this point, you may cover and set aside for up to 6 hours.)

While you cook ravioli, finish sauce. Add 1¼ cups **whipping cream** to basil mixture; bring to a boil over high heat. Reduce heat to low and add ½ cup (¼ lb.) **butter** or margarine all in one piece. Stir constantly until butter is smoothly blended into sauce.

Per serving: 635 calories, 18 g protein, 40 g carbohydrates, 46 g total fat, 231 mg cholesterol, 365 mg sodium

Scallop Ravioli

Follow directions for **Salmon Ravioli** (facing page), but use ½ pound **scallops** (rinsed and drained) in place of salmon in mousse. Omit Basil Sauce, sautéed tomato-garlic mixture, and basil sprigs. Accompany ravioli with this Tarragon-Saffron Sauce:

Tarragon-Saffron Sauce. Melt 1 tablespoon **butter** or margarine in a wide frying pan over medium-high heat. Stir in 1 tablespoon minced **shallot** and 1 tablespoon finely chopped **fresh tarragon leaves** (or ½ teaspoon dry tarragon). Add ¾ cup **dry white wine,** 1½ cups **regular-strength chicken broth,** and 1/32 teaspoon **ground saffron.**

Bring to a boil over high heat; boil, uncovered, until reduced by half. Add ½ cup **whipping cream** and boil rapidly until reduced to 1 cup. (At this point, you may cover sauce and set aside for up to 6 hours; reheat to continue.) Reduce heat to low and add ½ cup (¼ lb.) **butter** or margarine all in one piece. Stir constantly until butter is smoothly blended into sauce.

Tortellini with Monkfish & Gorgonzola

Preparation time: 15 to 20 minutes

Cooking time: About 40 minutes

Plump tortellini join a stir-fry of broccoli and monkfish in this appetizing main dish. Complementing the medley are a spunky cheese sauce and a sprinkling of toasted walnuts.

- 1 **pound monkfish fillet**
- 3 **tablespoons butter or margarine**
- ¾ **cup coarsely chopped walnuts**
- 5 **cups fresh broccoli flowerets**
- 1¼ **cups plus 2 tablespoons regular-strength chicken broth**
- 1 **package (7 oz.) dry cheese-stuffed tortellini**
- 1 **medium-size onion, finely chopped**
- 4 **teaspoons cornstarch**
- ½ **cup lightly packed crumbled Gorgonzola or other blue-veined cheese**
- ½ **teaspoon coarsely ground pepper**
- 1 **tablespoon white wine vinegar**

If necessary, remove silvery membrane from fish: slide a knife underneath membrane to loosen it, then pull it off from one side. Rinse fish and pat dry. Cut fish into bite-size ⅜- to ½-inch-thick slanting slices; set aside.

Melt 1 tablespoon of the butter in a wide frying pan over medium heat. Add walnuts and cook, stirring often, until crisp and lightly browned (8 to 10 minutes). Drain on paper towels and set aside.

Add 1 tablespoon more butter to pan; then add fish. Cook, stirring lightly, until just slightly translucent or wet inside; cut to test (about 3 minutes). Lift out fish and place in a bowl.

Add broccoli and 2 tablespoons of the broth to pan. Cover and cook, stirring once or twice, until broccoli is just tender when pierced (6 to 8 minutes). Lift out broccoli and add to fish.

While broccoli is cooking, in a 4- to 5-quart pan, cook tortellini in 3 quarts of boiling water just until tender to bite (12 to 15 minutes); or cook according to package directions. Drain well and set aside.

Rinse pan in which broccoli was cooked. Add remaining 1 tablespoon butter and melt over medium heat. Add onion and cook, stirring often, until soft (about 5 minutes). Sprinkle cornstarch over onion; stir until well coated. Remove from heat and gradually stir in remaining 1¼ cups broth; return to heat and continue to cook, stirring, until sauce boils and thickens. Reduce heat to low and mix in 6 tablespoons of the cheese; stir until melted. Mix in pepper; then add fish, broccoli, and tortellini. Mix gently until heated through (2 to 4 minutes). Stir in vinegar. Serve sprinkled with walnuts and remaining 2 tablespoons cheese. Makes 4 servings.

Per serving: 593 calories, 38 g protein, 38 g carbohydrates, 34 g total fat, 64 mg cholesterol, 934 mg sodium

Capellini with Tuna & Preserved Lemons

Preparation time: 15 minutes; 1 week for lemons to stand

Chilling time: 30 minutes

Cooking time: 8 to 10 minutes

Pickled lemons in oil contribute tart, salty flavor to strips of grilled tuna and delicate pasta. Each time you use the lemons, replenish the oil as needed—that way, you'll have enough to use in later recipes.

Preserved Lemons (recipe follows)
1 to 1½ pounds boneless and skinless fresh tuna, such as albacore, bluefin, or yellowfin (¾ to 1 inch thick)
1 tablespoon *each* drained capers and liquid from capers
¼ cup thinly sliced ripe olives
8 ounces dry capellini or fidelini

Prepare Preserved Lemons.

Rinse tuna and pat dry. Place in a shallow glass baking dish just large enough to hold fish in a single layer. Thinly slice 4 of the Preserved Lemon wedges; distribute over fish. Then spoon ¼ cup of the liquid from lemons over fish; turn fish to coat well. Cover and refrigerate for 30 minutes.

Remove fish from marinade and set aside; pour marinade into a small pan and add capers, caper liquid, and olives. Heat over low heat just until warm; keep warm.

Place fish on a well-greased grill about 6 inches above a solid bed of hot coals. Cook, turning once, until just slightly translucent or wet inside; cut in thickest part to test (3 to 4 minutes *total*). Keep hot.

In a 4- to 5-quart pan, cook capellini in 3 quarts of boiling water just until tender to bite (2 to 3 minutes); or cook according to package directions. Drain well; then mix with lemon sauce, lifting pasta lightly with 2 forks. Cut hot grilled tuna across the grain into ½-inch-wide strips and distribute over pasta. Serve at once. Makes 4 servings.

Preserved Lemons. Cut 2 **lemons** into 8 wedges each. Add 2½ tablespoons **kosher or coarse salt** and 1 teaspoon **sugar;** mix lightly. Place in a wide-mouth jar with a tight-fitting lid. Mix in ¼ cup **lemon juice,** cover tightly, and let stand at room temperature for 1 week, shaking jar once a day. Before using, mix in ½ cup **olive oil.** Stored in refrigerator, lemons will keep for up to 6 months; add more oil to jar as needed. Makes about 1¾ cups.

Per serving: 455 calories, 34 g protein, 45 g carbohydrates, 15 g total fat, 43 mg cholesterol, 915 mg sodium

Red & Black Lemon Pasta

Preparation time: 8 to 10 minutes

Cooking time: About 15 minutes

Chilling time: At least 1 hour

Glistening like jewels, beads of salmon and lumpfish caviar crown swirls of cold capellini in this colorful salad. A champagne dressing adds to the festive spirit.

1½ cups natural or brut champagne or dry white wine
3 strips lemon peel (yellow part only), *each* about ½ by 2½ inches
3 tablespoons salad oil
1 teaspoon white wine vinegar
⅛ teaspoon *each* ground white pepper and liquid hot pepper seasoning
4 ounces dry capellini or vermicelli
Salt
3 ounces red salmon caviar
1 tablespoon lumpfish caviar
Parsley sprigs
2 or 4 thin lemon wedges

In a 2- to 3-quart pan, bring champagne to a boil over high heat; boil, uncovered, until reduced to 3 tablespoons. Remove from heat. Cut lemon peel crosswise into very thin strips; add to reduced champagne along with oil, vinegar, pepper, and hot pepper seasoning. Set aside.

In a 4- to 5-quart pan, cook pasta in 2 quarts of boiling water just until tender to bite (2 to 3 minutes for capellini, 8 to 10 minutes for vermicelli); or cook according to package directions. Drain, rinse with cold water, and drain well again. Combine pasta with champagne mixture and mix lightly. Season to taste with salt. Cover and refrigerate until cold (at least 1 hour or up to 8 hours).

Divide pasta among individual plates. Place salmon caviar in a fine wire strainer and rinse under cold running water; drain well. Repeat to rinse lumpfish caviar. Sprinkle pasta with caviars, dividing evenly. Garnish each serving with parsley sprigs and a lemon wedge. Makes 4 first-course or 2 main-dish servings.

Per first-course serving: 263 calories, 10 g protein, 23 g carbohydrates, 15 g total fat, 149 mg cholesterol, 388 mg sodium

From the sprig of fresh basil on top to the bed of linguine beneath, Pasta with Shrimp in Tomato Cream (recipe on page 65) is a showy, savory treat. Complete the meal with a mixed green salad and crusty rolls.

A delicacy from the Northwest, wood-smoked salmon is firmer in texture and smokier in flavor than moist, buttery-rich lox. Its robust character has won it the respect of discerning cooks, who prize its unique contribution to a number of dishes.

Wood-smoked salmon is available from some fish markets fresh-smoked, but you can also purchase it frozen, vacuum-packed, or canned. (You may find it sold as *kippered, mild-cure,* or *Indian-type* salmon.) Once you've opened a package, store it in the refrigerator and plan to use it within a week.

Smoked Salmon Carbonara

    8 ounces dry vermicelli
    4 eggs
    ¼ cup chopped Italian parsley
    1 cup (about 5 oz.) grated Parmesan cheese
    1 tablespoon butter or margarine
    1 tablespoon olive oil
    1 medium-size onion, thinly sliced
    1 clove garlic, minced or pressed
    ¼ pound wood-smoked salmon, shredded or coarsely chopped (⅔ to 1 cup)
       Salt and coarsely ground pepper
       Grated Parmesan cheese (optional)

In a 5- to 6-quart pan, cook vermicelli in 3 quarts of boiling water just until tender to bite (8 to 10 minutes); or cook according to package directions.

Meanwhile, in a bowl beat eggs until well blended; mix in parsley and the 1 cup cheese. Set aside. Also melt butter in oil in a wide frying pan

Wood-Smoked Salmon

over medium-high heat. Add onion and cook, stirring often, until soft but not browned (5 to 6 minutes); stir in garlic.

Drain pasta well and add to onion mixture along with salmon. Cook, lifting the pasta lightly with 2 forks to mix, just until heated through (1 to 2 minutes).

Remove from heat and add egg mixture; continue to mix lightly with forks until pasta is coated with sauce. Season to taste with salt and pepper. Serve at once, with additional cheese, if desired. Makes 3 or 4 servings.

Per serving: 525 calories, 31 g protein, 46 g carbohydrates, 23 g total fat, 312 mg cholesterol, 892 mg sodium

Smoked Salmon & Red Onion Tart

       Rye Pastry (recipe follows)
    3 medium-size red onions (about 1¼ lbs. *total*)
    ¼ cup butter or margarine
    3 to 4 ounces wood-smoked salmon, flaked (½ to ⅔ cup)
    3 eggs
    1 cup half-and-half
    ¼ teaspoon salt
    ⅛ teaspoon *each* ground white pepper and ground nutmeg

Prepare Rye Pastry. Roll out on a floured surface to about a 13-inch circle. Ease into a 10-inch quiche dish; trim pastry even with rim of dish. Line pastry shell with foil, molding it against sides. Half-fill with raw beans, rice, or pie weights. Bake in a

425° oven for 10 minutes. Carefully lift out foil and beans; continue to bake pastry for 5 more minutes. Remove from oven, place on a rack, and reduce oven temperature to 350°.

While pastry is baking, cut off ends of onions. Cut each onion in half lengthwise, then thinly slice each half lengthwise so it falls into slivers. Melt butter in a wide frying pan over medium heat. Add onions and cook, stirring often, until soft and golden (15 to 20 minutes). Mix in flaked salmon, then spread mixture evenly in pastry shell.

In a bowl, beat eggs, half-and-half, salt, pepper, and nutmeg until well combined. Pour over onion mixture. Bake until custard is set and lightly browned (25 to 30 minutes). Let stand for 5 minutes; then cut into wedges. Makes 6 servings.

Rye Pastry. In a bowl, mix 1⅓ cups **all-purpose flour,** 3 tablespoons **rye flour,** and ¼ teaspoon **salt.** Add ⅓ cup firm **butter** or margarine (cut into pieces) and 2 tablespoons **solid vegetable shortening;** cut into flour mixture with a pastry blender or 2 knives until fine particles form. Add 1 **egg,** lightly beaten. Stir with a fork until dough clings together. With your hands, gather dough into a ball.

Per serving: 459 calories, 12 g protein, 32 g carbohydrates, 32 g total fat, 249 mg cholesterol, 537 mg sodium

Pictured on page 63
Pasta with Shrimp in Tomato Cream

Preparation time: 15 minutes

Cooking time: About 20 minutes

Slivered sun-dried tomatoes and large shrimp are stirred into a basil-seasoned cream sauce for tender linguine.

- ⅓ **cup dried tomatoes packed in oil**
- 1 **clove garlic, minced or pressed**
- 1 **pound medium-large raw shrimp (30 to 35 per lb.), shelled and deveined**
- ¼ **cup thinly sliced green onions (including tops)**
- 1½ **tablespoons chopped fresh basil leaves or 1 teaspoon dry basil leaves**
- ¼ **teaspoon ground white pepper**
- 1 **cup regular-strength chicken broth**
- ¾ **cup dry vermouth**
- 1 **cup whipping cream**
- 10 **ounces dry linguine**
     Fresh basil sprigs (optional)
     Grated Parmesan cheese

Drain tomatoes, reserving 2 tablespoons of the oil. Sliver tomatoes and set aside. Heat oil from tomatoes in a wide frying pan over medium-high heat. Add garlic and shrimp. Cook, stirring often, until shrimp are opaque throughout; cut to test (about 5 minutes). Lift out and set aside.

Add tomatoes, onions, chopped basil, pepper, broth, vermouth, and cream to pan. Bring to a boil over high heat; boil, stirring occasionally, until reduced to about 1½ cups (about 10 minutes). Return shrimp to pan and stir just until heated through.

Meanwhile, in a 4- to 5-quart pan, cook linguine in 3 quarts of boiling water just until tender to bite (8 to 10 minutes); or cook according to package directions. Drain pasta well, then divide among 4 dinner plates and top with sauce. Garnish with basil sprigs, if desired. Offer cheese to add to taste. Makes 4 servings.

Per serving: 631 calories, 30 g protein, 65 g carbohydrates, 28 g total fat, 206 mg cholesterol, 840 mg sodium

Garlic & Orange Sautéed Shrimp

Preparation time: About 25 minutes

Cooking time: About 20 minutes

Juicy colossal-size shrimp are the stars in this tempting entrée. Sauté the shellfish and mix them with a simple orange sauce, then cluster them in a starfish pattern atop a sea of capellini and fresh spinach.

- 8 **ounces dry capellini or fidelini**
- 2 **pounds spinach, rinsed well, stems removed**
- ¼ **cup butter or margarine**
- 3 **cloves garlic, minced or pressed**
- 1½ **tablespoons dry basil leaves**
- 20 **colossal raw shrimp (10 to 15 per lb.), shelled (except for tails) and deveined**
- 1 **teaspoon grated orange peel**
- 1½ **cups orange juice**
- 2 **tablespoons lemon juice**
- 1½ **tablespoons cornstarch**

In a 4- to 5-quart pan, cook pasta in 3 quarts of boiling water just until tender to bite (2 to 3 minutes); or cook according to package directions. Drain pasta well; then return to pan, cover, and keep warm.

Place about half the spinach (with water that clings to leaves) in a wide frying pan. Cover and cook over medium-high heat until wilted (about 4 minutes). Lift from pan, drain, and keep warm. Repeat with remaining spinach.

Melt butter in frying pan over medium heat. Add garlic and basil; cook, stirring often, until garlic is golden (1 to 2 minutes). Add shrimp and cook, turning once or twice, until opaque throughout; cut to test (5 to 7 minutes).

Meanwhile, stir together orange peel, orange juice, lemon juice, and cornstarch. Add to shrimp; cook, stirring, until sauce is thickened. Remove from heat. Lift out shrimp and set aside. Add pasta to sauce; mix lightly, using 2 forks.

Divide pasta equally among 4 warm dinner plates. Place a fourth of the spinach in the center of each serving of pasta. Arrange 5 shrimp, tails up, in a starfish pattern atop each portion of spinach. Makes 4 servings.

Per serving: 566 calories, 43 g protein, 65 g carbohydrates, 15 g total fat, 255 mg cholesterol, 469 mg sodium

A tangle of lemon zest flavors bright Scallops & Red Peppers with Linguine (recipe on facing page). Serve as an elegant first course; or team with crisp bread sticks and a marinated vegetable salad for a light supper.

Scallops & Red Peppers with Linguine

Preparation time: 25 to 30 minutes

Cooking time: 15 to 20 minutes

Sweet red peppers and succulent scallops mingle in a simple and colorful sauce for linguine. Serve as a first course or, in larger portions, as an entrée.

- 1 lemon
- 12 ounces dry linguine
- 1 pound sea scallops, rinsed and drained
- ¼ cup butter or margarine
- ¼ cup olive oil
- 3 large red bell peppers, seeded and cut into thin slivers
- 2 cloves garlic, minced or pressed
- ¼ to ½ teaspoon crushed red pepper
- ¾ cup regular-strength chicken broth
- ¾ cup finely chopped parsley
  Salt and pepper

Using a zester, cut peel (yellow part only) from lemon in fine shreds. (Or thinly pare off yellow part of peel and cut into thin slivers.) Set aside. Squeeze juice from lemon (you need ¼ cup); set aside.

In a 5- to 6-quart pan, cook linguine in 4 quarts of boiling water just until tender to bite (8 to 10 minutes); or cook according to package directions. Drain well and set aside.

Meanwhile, slice scallops ¼ inch thick and set aside. Melt butter in oil in a wide frying pan over medium-high heat. Add bell peppers, garlic, and crushed red pepper, then cook, stirring, for 1 minute. Lift out bell peppers with a slotted spoon; keep warm. Add broth and lemon juice to pan and bring to a boil. Add scallops, cover, and cook until scallops are opaque throughout; cut to test (2 to 3 minutes). Remove from heat. Lift out scallops with a slotted spoon and add to bell pepper mixture.

Add pasta to pan, then heat, mixing lightly with 2 forks, until pasta is hot. Transfer pasta and sauce to a warm serving dish, then top with parsley, scallop-pepper mixture, and lemon peel. Mix lightly; season to taste with salt and pepper. Makes 6 first-course or 3 or 4 main-dish servings.

Per first-course serving: 447 calories, 21 g protein, 49 g carbohydrates, 18 g total fat, 46 mg cholesterol, 331 mg sodium

Scallops & Green Noodles

Preparation time: About 25 minutes

Cooking time: 12 to 15 minutes

Barely cooked slivers of carrot, bell pepper, and green onion add color and a crisp texture to this creamy blend of spinach noodles and scallops. The pasta readily absorbs the delicate yet distinctive flavor of the shellfish, especially when they're thinly sliced.

- 2 large carrots
- 1 large red bell pepper, quartered and seeded
- 8 green onions (including tops)
- 1 pound sea scallops, rinsed and drained
- ½ cup (¼ lb.) butter or margarine
- ⅔ cup dry white wine
- 1½ cups whipping cream
- 8 ounces dry spinach egg noodles
  Salt and pepper
  Freshly grated nutmeg

Cut carrots, bell pepper, and onions into slivers ⅛ inch thick and 2 to 3 inches long. Set aside in separate piles. Slice scallops ¼ inch thick; set aside.

Melt 2 tablespoons of the butter in a wide frying pan over high heat. Add carrots and cook, stirring, until slightly limp (about 1 minute); lift out and set aside. Add 1 tablespoon more butter and bell pepper; cook, stirring, until slightly limp (about 1 minute). Lift out and add to carrots. Add onions and 1 tablespoon more butter; stir just until hot (30 to 45 seconds). Add to carrots and pepper. Set aside.

Add wine to pan and bring to a boil. Add scallops, reduce heat, cover, and simmer until scallops are opaque throughout; cut to test (2 to 3 minutes). Lift scallops from pan with a slotted spoon and add to vegetables; keep warm. Add cream to liquid in pan, increase heat to high, and bring to a full boil. Boil, uncovered, until reduced to 1¾ cups. Reduce heat to low; add remaining ¼ cup butter and stir until smoothly blended into sauce.

While you are finishing sauce, in a 5- to 6-quart pan, cook noodles in 4 quarts of boiling water just until tender to bite (5 to 7 minutes); or cook according to package directions. Drain well.

Add noodles to hot cream sauce; mix lightly with 2 forks. Add scallops and vegetables and mix gently. Season to taste with salt, pepper, and nutmeg. Makes 4 to 6 servings.

Per serving: 548 calories, 20 g protein, 36 g carbohydrates, 36 g total fat, 168 mg cholesterol, 314 mg sodium

8 to 10 minutes for dry); or cook according to package directions. Drain well.

Spoon crab sauce over pasta; mix lightly, using 2 forks. Makes 4 first-course or 2 main-dish servings.

Per first-course serving: 411 calories, 18 g protein, 35 g carbohydrates, 22 g total fat, 112 mg cholesterol, 228 mg sodium

■ *To Microwave:* In a 2-quart microwave-safe casserole, combine butter, oil, onions, garlic, tomatoes, and wine. Microwave, uncovered, on **HIGH (100%)** for 4 to 6 minutes or until mixture boils all over. Meanwhile, cook fettuccine as directed. To tomato mixture, add lemon juice, crab, and parsley. Cover and microwave on **HIGH (100%)** for 1 to 2 minutes or until crab is heated through. Season and serve as directed.

Fettuccine with Crab

Preparation time: About 15 minutes

Cooking time: 5 to 12 minutes

Laden with fresh crab, this fresh tomato and white wine sauce is a worthy topping for your own fresh fettuccine. (It's just as good on purchased pasta.)

- 2 tablespoons butter or margarine
- ¼ cup olive oil or salad oil
- ½ cup thinly sliced green onions (including tops)
- 1 clove garlic, minced or pressed
- 2 medium-size tomatoes, peeled, seeded, and chopped
- ¼ cup dry white wine
- 1 tablespoon lemon juice
- ½ pound cooked crabmeat
- ¼ cup finely chopped parsley
  Salt and freshly ground pepper
- 8 ounces fresh or 6 ounces dry fettuccine

Melt butter in oil in a wide frying pan over medium heat. Add onions, garlic, tomatoes, and wine. Bring to a boil, stirring often. Boil gently for 2 minutes. Add lemon juice, crab, and parsley. Stir gently just until crab is heated through. Season to taste with salt and pepper; keep warm.

While you are preparing sauce, in a 4- to 5-quart pan, cook fettuccine in 3 quarts of boiling water just until tender to bite (2 to 3 minutes for fresh pasta,

Creamy Lasagne with Crab & Shrimp

Preparation time: About 35 minutes

Cooking time: 15 to 20 minutes

Baking time: 40 to 45 minutes

A good choice for entertaining, this delicate seafood version of a popular pasta dish features two favorite shellfish in a wine and cream sauce.

- ⅓ cup butter or margarine
- 1 cup thinly sliced green onions (including tops)
- 1 clove garlic, minced or pressed
- ½ teaspoon dry tarragon
- 1½ pounds medium-size raw shrimp (30 to 50 per lb.), shelled and deveined
- ⅓ cup all-purpose flour
- 1 cup *each* whipping cream and regular-strength chicken broth
- ½ cup dry vermouth or white wine
- 1 package (8 oz.) dry lasagne noodles
- ½ pound cooked crabmeat
- 2 cups (8 oz.) shredded Jarlsberg or Swiss cheese

Melt 1 tablespoon of the butter in a wide frying pan over medium heat. Add onions, garlic, and tarragon; cook, stirring, for 1 minute. Add shrimp and cook, stirring often, until opaque throughout; cut to test (3 to 4 minutes). Spoon shrimp mixture into a bowl and set aside.

Melt remaining butter in pan over medium heat. Add flour and stir until bubbly. Remove from heat and mix in cream, broth, and vermouth. Increase heat to medium-high and bring to a boil, stirring constantly; set aside.

In a 6-quart pan, cook lasagne in 4 quarts of boiling water just until tender to bite (about 10 minutes); or cook according to package directions. Drain, rinse with cold water until cool, and drain well again. Set aside.

Spoon off any accumulated juices from shrimp mixture; stir juices into sauce.

Line a greased 9- by 13-inch baking dish with a third of the lasagne. Layer with a third each of the sauce, shrimp mixture, crab, and cheese. Repeat, making 2 more layers each of noodles, sauce, shrimp, crab, and cheese. Cover. (At this point, you may refrigerate for up to a day.)

Bake, covered, in a 350° oven for 20 minutes. Uncover and continue to bake until golden and bubbly (20 to 25 more minutes). Makes 6 to 8 servings.

Per serving: 502 calories, 33 g protein, 31 g carbohydrates, 27 g total fat, 213 mg cholesterol, 471 mg sodium

Pilaf del Mar

Preparation time: 15 to 20 minutes

Cooking time: About 30 minutes

A variety of white-fleshed fish—fresh or frozen—can go into the delicious marinara sauce for this herb-flavored rice pilaf.

    Herbed Pilaf (recipe follows)
- 1 pound skinless white-fleshed fish fillets, such as cod, orange roughy, halibut, or rockfish
- 2 tablespoons olive oil or salad oil
- 1 medium-size onion, finely chopped
- 1 clove garlic, minced or pressed
- ¼ pound mushrooms, thinly sliced
- 1 small green bell pepper, seeded and finely chopped
- 1 can (about 1 lb.) tomatoes
- 2 teaspoons dry basil leaves
- 1 tablespoon *each* Worcestershire and tomato paste
- ¼ cup dry white wine
- ¼ cup finely chopped parsley
    Salt and pepper

Prepare Herbed Pilaf.

While pilaf is cooking, rinse fish, pat dry, and cut into bite-size pieces; remove any small bones. Set aside.

Heat oil in a wide frying pan over medium heat; add onion, garlic, and mushrooms. Cook, stirring often, until onion is soft (about 5 minutes). Add bell pepper and increase heat to medium-high; cook, stirring often, until almost all liquid has evaporated. Add tomatoes (break up with a spoon) and their liquid, basil, Worcestershire, tomato paste, and wine; cook, stirring often, until sauce is thick (8 to 10 minutes).

Add fish to sauce. Reduce heat, cover, and simmer until fish is just slightly translucent or wet inside; cut in thickest part to test (6 to 8 minutes). Stir in parsley and season to taste with salt and pepper. Serve over Herbed Pilaf. Makes 4 servings.

Herbed Pilaf. Heat 2 tablespoons **olive oil** in a 2- to 2½-quart pan over medium heat. Add 1 small **onion,** finely chopped, and 1 cup **long-grain white rice.** Cook, stirring often, until rice looks opaque (3 to 4 minutes). Stir in 1 teaspoon **herbes de Provence** or Italian herb seasoning and 1 clove **garlic,** minced or pressed. Then add 1 cup **Fish Stock,** page 37 (or one 8-ounce bottle clam juice), and 1 cup **dry white wine.** Reduce heat, cover, and simmer until rice is tender to bite and liquid is absorbed (20 to 25 minutes).

Per serving: 440 calories, 26 g protein, 50 g carbohydrates, 15 g total fat, 49 mg cholesterol, 459 mg sodium

Royal Scallop
& Shrimp Curry

Preparation time: About 15 minutes

Cooking time: About 15 minutes

Fluffy steamed rice is the perfect foil for a classic, creamy seafood curry. Use Madras curry powder if you can find it—it's sold in spice shops and some supermarkets.

Many curry lovers enjoy beer with this kind of dish; if you prefer wine, try a spicy Alsace-style Gewürztraminer.

- ¼ **cup butter or margarine**
- 1 **small onion, finely chopped**
- 2 **cloves garlic, minced or pressed**
- 1 **to 2 teaspoons Madras curry powder or 2 to 3 teaspoons regular curry powder**
- ¾ **pound sea scallops, rinsed and drained**
- 1 **pound medium-size raw shrimp (30 to 50 per lb.), shelled and deveined**
- 1 **cup whipping cream**
- ½ **cup dry white wine**
- ½ **teaspoon dry summer savory**
- 1 **tablespoon cornstarch blended with 2 tablespoons water**
  Salt and pepper
  Hot cooked rice

Melt 2 tablespoons of the butter in a wide frying pan over medium heat; add onion, garlic, and curry powder. Cook, stirring often, until onion is soft (about 5 minutes). Add remaining 2 tablespoons butter and stir until melted. Add scallops and shrimp. Cook, stirring often, until scallops and shrimp are opaque throughout; cut one of each to test (3 to 5 minutes). Lift out shellfish with a slotted spoon and keep warm.

Remove pan from heat and stir in cream, wine, savory, and cornstarch mixture. Return to heat and continue to cook, stirring constantly, until sauce boils and thickens. Then add shellfish and any accumulated juices; stir gently until heated through. Season to taste with salt and pepper. Serve over rice. Makes 4 to 6 servings.

Per serving: 311 calories, 23 g protein, 6 g carbohydrates, 22 g total fat, 177 mg cholesterol, 275 mg sodium

---

Pictured on facing page

Shrimp Pilaf

Preparation time: About 30 minutes

Cooking time: 35 to 40 minutes

Pilaf is a Mideast rice dish that's prepared in countless variations. Cook this colorful shrimp version in an attractive pan that can go straight from rangetop to table.

- 6 **tablespoons butter or margarine**
- 1 **pound large raw shrimp (under 30 per lb.), shelled and deveined**
- 1 **bottle (8 oz.) clam juice**
- 1 **medium-size onion, thinly sliced**
- 2 **cloves garlic, minced or pressed**
- 1 **cup long-grain white rice**
- 1 **teaspoon ground turmeric**
- 1 **cup thinly sliced celery**
- ½ **teaspoon salt**
- ¼ **teaspoon pepper**
- 2 **medium-size tomatoes, peeled and chopped**
- 1 **package (10 oz.) frozen tiny peas, thawed**
  Chopped parsley

[handwritten: 5 lbs → gr. chiles]

Melt 2 tablespoons of the butter in a deep, heavy 4- to 5-quart pan over medium heat. Add shrimp and cook, stirring, until almost opaque throughout; cut to test (3 to 4 minutes). Lift out and set aside. Pour pan juices into a 1-quart measure; add clam juice and enough water to make 2½ cups. Set aside.

Melt remaining ¼ cup butter in pan over medium heat. Add onion and garlic. Cook, stirring often, until onion is soft (about 5 minutes). Add rice and turmeric; cook, stirring, for 2 to 3 minutes. Add celery, salt, pepper, and clam juice mixture. Reduce heat, cover, and simmer until rice is almost tender to bite (about 15 minutes).

With a fork, lightly mix tomatoes and peas into rice; scatter shrimp over top. Cover and continue to cook until rice is tender to bite and liquid is absorbed (about 10 more minutes). Sprinkle with parsley. Makes 4 to 6 servings.

Per serving: 329 calories, 18 g protein, 35 g carbohydrates, 13 g total fat, 124 mg cholesterol, 563 mg sodium

A meal-in-a-pan reminiscent of paella, Shrimp Pilaf
(recipe on facing page) includes golden rice, fresh tomatoes, and peas. Complement its vibrant flavors with
warm garlic bread and a green salad.

Risotto & Shrimp Primavera

Preparation time: About 20 minutes

Cooking time: About 40 minutes

Creamy rice and pink shrimp contrast with the vivid colors and bolder flavors of tender-crisp spring vegetables in this luscious main dish.

- 1 cup Chinese pea pods (also called snow or sugar peas) or sugar snap peas
- 8 asparagus spears
- 1 small carrot
- 3½ cups regular-strength chicken broth
- 3 tablespoons butter or margarine
- 2 tablespoons olive oil
- 1 small onion, finely chopped
- 1 small clove garlic, minced or pressed
- 1 cup short-grain rice (such as pearl)
- ½ pound tiny cooked and shelled shrimp
- ½ cup whipping cream
- ½ cup freshly grated Parmesan cheese
- ⅛ teaspoon ground white pepper
  Salt (optional)
- 2 tablespoons 1-inch-long chive strips

Break off ends of pea pods; remove and discard strings. Cut pods on the diagonal into ¾-inch-wide strips. Snap off and discard tough ends of asparagus; cut stems diagonally into ½-inch slices and set tips aside. Thinly slice carrot on the diagonal.

In a 2-quart pan, bring 1 cup of the broth to a boil over high heat. Add pea pods and cook just until broth returns to a boil; remove from heat, lift out pea pods with a slotted spoon, and place them in a bowl. Return broth to a boil; add asparagus tips and sliced stems. Cook just until broth returns to a boil; remove from heat, lift out asparagus, and add to pea pods in bowl. Return broth to a boil; add carrot, return to a boil, and boil for 2 minutes. Lift out carrot and add to pea pods and asparagus. Reserve broth.

Melt 2 tablespoons of the butter in oil in a heavy 2- to 2½-quart pan over medium heat. Add onion and cook, stirring, until soft and golden (about 5 minutes). Add garlic and rice and stir until rice looks opaque (about 3 minutes).

Mix in remaining 2½ cups broth, plus broth in which vegetables were blanched. Cook, stirring occasionally, until mixture comes to a boil. Adjust heat so mixture boils gently. Cook, uncovered, stirring occasionally at first and then more often to prevent scorching as liquid is absorbed, until rice is almost tender to bite (18 to 20 minutes).

Stir in pea pods, asparagus, carrot, shrimp, and cream. Continue to cook until rice is just tender to bite without tasting starchy and mixture is moist but not soupy (2 to 4 more minutes). Stir in remaining 1 tablespoon butter, ¼ cup of the cheese, and pepper. Season to taste with salt, if desired. Serve sprinkled with chives and remaining ¼ cup cheese. Makes 4 servings.

Per serving: 577 calories, 25 g protein, 50 g carbohydrates, 31 g total fat, 177 mg cholesterol, 1,340 mg sodium

Indonesian Grilled Shrimp with Yellow Rice

Preparation time: About 30 minutes

Chilling time: At least 4 hours

Cooking time: 20 to 25 minutes

A scaled-down version of Indonesia's renowned *rijsttafel*, this spicy shrimp entrée is served on a bed of golden rice and surrounded by an array of condiments for guests to add as they please.

- 1 medium-size onion, cut into chunks
- 3 or 4 cloves garlic
- 3 tablespoons sugar
- 2 tablespoons *each* salted roasted peanuts and soy sauce
- 1½ teaspoons pepper
- 1 teaspoon grated lemon peel
- 1 teaspoon Chinese five-spice; or ¼ teaspoon *each* ground allspice, crushed anise seeds, ground cinnamon, ground cloves, and ground ginger
- 1 to 1½ pounds large raw shrimp (under 30 per lb.), shelled and deveined
  Indonesian Yellow Rice (recipe on facing page)
  Condiments (suggestions on facing page)

In a food processor or blender, combine onion, garlic, sugar, peanuts, soy sauce, pepper, lemon peel, and five-spice. Whirl until almost smooth. Place shrimp in a glass bowl; pour onion mixture over them. Cover and refrigerate for at least 4 hours or until next day.

Remove shrimp from marinade, reserving marinade. Thread shrimp close together on thin metal skewers, inserting skewers through centers of shrimp.

Prepare Indonesian Yellow Rice. When rice is almost done, grill shrimp: place skewered shrimp on a greased grill 4 to 6 inches above a solid bed of hot coals. Cook, turning once and brushing with marinade, until shrimp are opaque throughout; cut to test (3 to 4 minutes *total*).

Mound Indonesian Yellow Rice into a cone in center of a platter. Surround with skewered shrimp. Serve with condiments to add to taste. Makes 6 servings.

Indonesian Yellow Rice. In a 3- to 4-quart pan, combine 4½ cups **water,** 1 cup **sweetened flaked coconut,** 2½ teaspoons **ground turmeric,** peel (yellow part only) pared from 1 **lemon,** 1 thin quarter-size slice **fresh ginger,** and 1 **bay leaf.** Bring to a boil over high heat; stir in 2¼ cups **long-grain white rice.** Reduce heat to low, cover, and simmer until rice is tender to bite (20 to 25 minutes). Remove and discard lemon peel, ginger, and bay leaf. Season to taste with **salt,** fluffing the rice with a fork.

Condiments. Choose at least 4 of the following: **tomato** wedges, **cucumber** spears, sliced **mango or papaya,** sliced **banana, lemon** wedges, **soy sauce,** and **crushed red pepper.**

Per serving: 434 calories, 19 g protein, 73 g carbohydrates, 7 g total fat, 93 mg cholesterol, 497 mg sodium

Tomato Risotto with Fresh Clam Sauce

Preparation time: About 15 minutes

Cooking time: 40 to 45 minutes

You've probably already enjoyed this classic white clam sauce over linguine—but you'll find it just as superb a complement for a rosy fresh tomato risotto.

	Fresh Clam Sauce (recipe follows)
3	tablespoons olive oil
1	medium onion, finely chopped
1½	cups short-grain rice (such as pearl)
1	clove garlic, minced or pressed
1	teaspoon dry basil leaves
1	small tomato, finely chopped
1	can (8 oz.) tomato sauce
1¼	cups dry white wine
2	cups regular-strength chicken broth

Prepare Fresh Clam Sauce. Heat oil in a deep, wide frying pan over medium heat. Add onion and cook, stirring often, until slightly golden (4 to 6 minutes). Add rice; cook, stirring often, until most of rice is opaque (3 to 4 minutes).

Mix in garlic, basil, tomato, tomato sauce, wine, and broth; increase heat to high and bring mixture to a boil. Then reduce heat and boil gently, uncovered, stirring occasionally at first and then more often to prevent scorching as liquid is absorbed, until rice is just tender to bite without tasting starchy (20 to 25 minutes). Spoon Fresh Clam Sauce over each portion. Makes 4 servings.

Fresh Clam Sauce. Scrub 3 to 4 dozen **small hard-shell clams in shells,** suitable for steaming. Pour ¼ cup **water** into a 4- to 5-quart pan. Add clams, cover and boil over medium-high heat just until shells open (5 to 10 minutes); remove clams as they open. Strain steaming liquid through several thicknesses of dampened cheesecloth to remove grit; reserve liquid. Discard any unopened clams; remove remaining clams from shells and set aside.

Melt 2 tablespoons **butter** or margarine in 2 tablespoons **olive oil** in a wide frying pan over medium heat. Add 1 small **onion,** finely chopped; cook, stirring often, until soft (about 5 minutes). Mix in 3 cloves **garlic,** minced or pressed, ½ cup **dry white wine,** and strained clam liquid. Bring to a boil, stirring occasionally; boil until almost all liquid has evaporated. Remove from heat.

Before serving, return to medium heat. Add clams and any juices; heat through. Season with **salt** and **pepper.** Stir in ½ cup chopped **parsley.**

Per serving: 632 calories, 25 g protein, 75 g carbohydrates, 26 g total fat, 61 mg cholesterol, 994 mg sodium

Deveining Shrimp

To devein shelled shrimp, make a ¼-inch-deep cut along the back with a sharp knife or scissors. Rinse out the vein under cool running water; or use a skewer to lift out the vein in several places along the back. If you wish to butterfly the deveined shrimp, split them along the vein, cutting almost all the way through to make the shrimp lie flat.

To devein unshelled shrimp, insert a pick or skewer between the shell segments in several places along the back to lift out the vein.

*Show off your silvery catch in Trout with Vegetable Stew
(recipe on page 85), a striking entrée for three. Accompany with sliced potatoes au gratin and a blush wine
such as white Zinfandel.*

Main Dishes

If, like many people, you're cooking more seafood now than you did a few years ago, you've probably discovered how fish and shellfish can expand your culinary horizons. Markets today offer marvelous choices that may be new to you—skate, monkfish, orange roughy, and catfish, for example. You'll find myriad ways to present seafood, too. Pass up the familiar tartar sauce and master a delicate *beurre blanc* to drizzle over sautéed or grilled fish and shellfish. Or try an adventurous flavor combination—perhaps Sole with Cranberry Butter Sauce or Flash-in–the-Pan Shrimp & Spinach with seedless grapes. All told, there are almost as many delicious seafood entrées as there are fish in the sea!

Mousse-topped Baked Salmon Steaks

Preparation time: 8 to 10 minutes

Baking time: About 15 minutes

Cooking time: About 5 minutes

Salmon steaks crowned with puffy mounds of gold-tinged fish mousse make a showy entrée you can assemble in advance. Serve the salmon and its delicate butter sauce with crunchy Chinese pea pods and tiny carrots.

- ½ **pound skinless white-fleshed fish fillets, such as cod, lingcod, or sole**
- 4 **salmon steaks (6 to 8 oz. *each*), 1 inch thick**
- 1 **egg**
- ½ **cup whipping cream**
- 1 **cup dry white wine**
- ½ **teaspoon dry thyme leaves**
- 1 **green onion (including top), thinly sliced**
- ¼ **cup butter or margarine, cut into 2 or 3 pieces**
  Salt and pepper
  Watercress sprigs

Rinse white-fleshed fish and salmon steaks, then pat dry. Arrange salmon steaks side by side in a 9- by 13-inch baking dish; set aside.

Cut white-fleshed fish into chunks and remove any small bones. Then whirl fish in a food processor until puréed (or put through a food chopper fitted with the fine blade). Add egg and ¼ cup of the cream; whirl (or mix with a spoon) until thoroughly blended. Spread fish mousse evenly over salmon steaks. (At this point, you may cover and refrigerate for up to 6 hours.)

Just before baking, pour wine around salmon. Bake, uncovered, in a 450° oven until mousse is delicately browned and salmon is just slightly translucent or wet inside; cut in thickest part to test (about 15 minutes).

With a slotted spatula, carefully transfer salmon to warm plates and keep warm. Pour cooking liquid from baking dish through a fine wire strainer into a wide frying pan. Add remaining ¼ cup cream, thyme, and onion; bring to a boil over high heat. Boil, stirring constantly, until sauce is reduced to ½ cup.

Reduce heat to low. Using a wire whisk, stir in butter, one piece at a time, until sauce is well blended, smooth, and thickened. Season to taste with salt and pepper. Spoon sauce around salmon; garnish each serving with a cluster of watercress sprigs. Makes 4 servings.

Per serving: 502 calories, 46 g protein, 2 g carbohydrates, 34 g total fat, 256 mg cholesterol, 256 mg sodium

Salmon with Egg-Cheese Mask

Preparation time: About 10 minutes

Baking & broiling time: 18 to 20 minutes

As the name of the dish implies, this big baked salmon fillet is completely covered with a "mask" of beaten eggs and two cheeses. The result? Perfectly cooked fish, with all its succulence and flavor sealed in.

- 1 salmon fillet (2½ to 2¾ lbs.)
- 3 tablespoons lemon or lime juice
  Freshly ground pepper
- 3 eggs
- 1 tablespoon chopped fresh dill or 1 teaspoon dry dill weed
- 1 cup (4 oz.) shredded mozzarella cheese
- ¾ cup freshly grated Parmesan cheese
  Thin lemon slices

Rinse salmon and pat dry. Place, skin side down, in a greased shallow rectangular or oval baking dish (about 9 by 13 inches). Drizzle lemon juice evenly over fish; sprinkle lightly with pepper.

Bake, uncovered, in a 400° oven until fish is just slightly translucent or wet inside; cut in thickest part to test (11 to 13 minutes).

Meanwhile, in bowl of an electric mixer, beat eggs at high speed until foamy and doubled in volume; beat in dill.

Remove fish from oven and sprinkle evenly with mozzarella cheese and ½ cup of the Parmesan cheese. Spread beaten eggs over fish to cover completely. Return to oven and continue to bake until egg mixture looks set when dish is gently shaken (about 5 more minutes). Remove from oven and sprinkle with remaining ¼ cup Parmesan cheese.

Broil 2 inches below heat until golden brown (about 3 minutes). Garnish with lemon slices. To serve, slice fish crosswise into strips; lift from dish with a wide spatula. Makes 6 to 8 servings.

Per serving: 314 calories, 37 g protein, 1 g carbohydrates, 17 g total fat, 199 mg cholesterol, 313 mg sodium

Pictured on page 87

Walla Walla Salmon

Preparation time: About 10 minutes

Cooking time: 25 to 30 minutes

Broiling time: 6 to 8 minutes

In the Pacific Northwest, imaginative cooks embellish local salmon with a variety of tempting toppings. Here, almonds, coconut, and sweet onions simmered in teriyaki sauce provide the finishing touches.

- ¼ cup sliced almonds
- ¼ cup sweetened shredded coconut
  Teriyaki Sauce (recipe follows)
- 1 tablespoon salad oil
- 2 large mild onions, thinly sliced
- 4 pieces salmon fillet (6 oz. *each*)
  Lemon wedges

Toast almonds in a wide frying pan over medium-low heat until light gold (about 6 minutes), stirring occasionally. Add coconut and stir until toasted (2 to 3 minutes). Remove almonds and coconut from pan and set aside.

Prepare Teriyaki Sauce. In pan, combine oil, onions, and 3 tablespoons of the Teriyaki Sauce. Cook over medium heat, stirring often, until onions are very soft (15 to 20 minutes).

Rinse salmon and pat dry. Brush some of the remaining Teriyaki Sauce over both sides of each piece. Place, skin side up, on a greased rack in a broiler pan. Broil 3 to 4 inches below heat, turning once and brushing with remaining Teriyaki Sauce, until fish is just slightly translucent or wet inside; cut in thickest part to test (6 to 8 minutes *total*).

To serve, top with onion mixture, almonds, and coconut. Garnish with lemon wedges. Makes 4 servings.

Teriyaki Sauce. Mix 3 tablespoons **soy sauce,** 2 tablespoons **dry sherry** or water, and 1 tablespoon *each* **Oriental sesame oil** and minced **fresh ginger.**

Per serving: 397 calories, 37 g protein, 11 g carbohydrates, 22 g total fat, 94 mg cholesterol, 861 mg sodium

Baked Fish, Mexican Style

Preparation time: About 5 minutes

Baking time: 12 to 15 minutes

Bound to become a family favorite, these fish steaks are baked with two popular snack foods—zesty salsa and crunchy corn chips. Preparation and cooking are both so quick that you can have dinner on the table in under half an hour.

- 1½ pounds boneless and skinless firm-textured fish steaks or fillets, such as mahi mahi, shark, or swordfish (about ¾ inch thick)
- 1 cup prepared tomato-based salsa
- 1 cup (4 oz.) shredded sharp Cheddar cheese
- ½ cup coarsely crushed corn chips
- 1 small firm-ripe avocado
  Sour cream (optional)
  Lime wedges

Rinse fish and pat dry; then place pieces side by side in an ungreased 8- by 12-inch baking dish. Pour salsa over fish. Sprinkle evenly with cheese, then with corn chips.

Bake, uncovered, in a 400° oven until fish is just slightly translucent or wet inside; cut in thickest part to test (12 to 15 minutes). Meanwhile, pit, peel, and slice avocado.

Garnish fish with avocado slices. Serve with sour cream, if desired; offer lime wedges to squeeze over fish to taste. Makes 4 servings.

Per serving: 397 calories, 40 g protein, 13 g carbohydrates, 20 g total fat, 154 mg cholesterol, 986 mg sodium

Skate with Browned Butter & Cabbage

Preparation time: About 10 minutes

Cooking time: 10 to 18 minutes

Long a favorite in France, skate (also called ray) is a surprising discovery to many on this side of the Atlantic. Serve the moist, delicately flavored fish over stir-fried cabbage, with a buttery sauce.

- 1 pound filleted or 1¼ pounds unfilleted skate, cut into 3 or 4 equal-size pieces
  All-purpose flour
- ¼ cup butter or margarine
- 1 tablespoon salad oil
- 2 tablespoons finely chopped shallots
- 1 small tomato, seeded and chopped
- 1 quart coarsely shredded cabbage
  Salt and pepper
- 1 tablespoon *each* lemon juice and chopped parsley

Rinse fish, pat dry, and dust lightly with flour. Melt 1 tablespoon of the butter in oil in a wide frying pan over medium-high heat. Add fish. Cook, turning once, until browned on outside and no longer translucent inside; cut in thickest part to test. Allow 5 to 8 minutes *total* for ¼- to 1-inch-thick fillets, 8 to 12 minutes *total* for unfilleted pieces ½ to 1¼ inches thick. Remove fish from pan and keep warm.

To pan, add shallots, tomato, and 1 tablespoon more butter. Cook, stirring, for 1 minute; then stir in cabbage. Stir-fry until cabbage is just tender-crisp to bite (2 to 2½ minutes). Season to taste with salt and pepper. Spoon cabbage onto a warm platter, top with fish, and keep warm.

Add remaining 2 tablespoons butter to pan; heat until butter foams and begins to brown. Remove from heat and stir in lemon juice and parsley. Spoon butter mixture over fish and cabbage. Makes 3 or 4 servings.

Per serving: 283 calories, 26 g protein, 9 g carbohydrates, 16 g total fat, 93 mg cholesterol, 213 mg sodium

Understanding Skate

The edible portions of skate are the triangular "wings." They're covered with a thick, slippery skin, usually removed before the fish is offered for sale at the market.

Skinned wings can be cooked whole or cut into fillets; each wing yields 2 fillets, divided from each other by cartilage. To fillet a wing, start at the thick side and run a sharp knife between the flesh and cartilage; repeat on the other side. Lift off the fillets and discard the cartilage. Divide the fillets into serving-size pieces.

Pictured on page 2

Sole with Cranberry Butter Sauce

Preparation time: About 5 minutes

Cooking time: 12 to 15 minutes

Tart, rosy-hued butter sauce made with fresh or frozen cranberries is a nice foil for delicate sautéed sole fillets. Serve with steamed baby carrots and pattypan squash, if you like.

   3 **tablespoons sugar**
   1 **cup fresh or frozen cranberries**
  ½ **teaspoon ground coriander**
  ¼ **teaspoon fennel seeds, coarsely crushed**
   1 **cup regular-strength chicken broth**
   1 **pound sole or flounder fillets (¼ to ⅓ inch thick)**
      All-purpose flour
  ½ **cup (¼ lb.) butter or margarine**
   2 **to 3 tablespoons salad oil**
  ⅓ **cup minced shallots**
      Fresh chervil or parsley sprigs

In a 1- to 1½-quart pan, combine sugar, cranberries, coriander, fennel seeds, and broth. Bring to a boil over high heat; cover, remove from heat, and set aside.

Rinse fish, pat dry, and dust lightly with flour. Melt 1½ tablespoons of the butter in 1½ tablespoons of the oil in a wide frying pan over medium-high heat. Add about half the fish (do not crowd in pan). Cook, turning once, until just slightly translucent or wet inside; cut in thickest part to test (2 to 3 minutes *total*). Transfer to a warm serving dish and keep warm. Repeat to cook remaining fish, adding more butter and oil as needed.

Reduce heat to medium. Add shallots and 1 tablespoon more butter to pan; cook, stirring, until shallots begin to soften (2 to 3 minutes). Add cranberry mixture, increase heat to high, and boil, uncovered, until reduced to ¾ cup.

Reduce heat to low. Add remaining butter (about 5 tablespoons) all in one piece and stir constantly until sauce is well blended, smooth, and thickened. Spoon sauce over fish, garnish with chervil sprigs, and serve immediately. Makes 4 servings.

Per serving: 463 calories, 23 g protein, 22 g carbohydrates, 32 g total fat, 117 mg cholesterol, 579 mg sodium

Pictured on facing page

Sesame-crusted Sea Bass with Zucchini

Preparation time: About 15 minutes

Cooking time: 15 to 20 minutes

Thin slivers of zucchini encircle sesame-crunchy fish fillets in this quick but stylish dinner.

   2 **pounds boneless and skinless sea bass or grouper fillets (¾ to 1 inch thick), cut into 4 to 6 equal-size pieces**
      Salt and ground white pepper
      All-purpose flour
  ½ **cup sesame seeds**
   1 **egg beaten with 2 tablespoons milk**
   6 **tablespoons butter or margarine**
   1 **tablespoon salad oil**
   3 **medium-size zucchini, cut into julienne strips**
   2 **tablespoons finely chopped shallots**
  ½ **cup dry vermouth**

Rinse fish and pat dry. Sprinkle lightly with salt and pepper, then dust lightly with flour. Spread sesame seeds on wax paper. Dip fish in egg mixture; drain briefly, then turn in sesame seeds to coat evenly. Set aside.

Melt 1 tablespoon of the butter in oil in a wide frying pan over medium heat. Add fish. Cook, turning once, until golden brown on outside and just slightly translucent or wet inside; cut in thickest part to test (6 to 10 minutes *total*). Transfer fish to a warm platter and keep warm.

Add zucchini and 1 tablespoon more butter to pan. Cook, stirring often, just until zucchini is tender-crisp to bite (2 to 3 minutes). Drain off and reserve any juices that have accumulated around fish; then spoon zucchini around fish.

To pan, add fish juices, shallots, and vermouth. Increase heat to high, bring to a boil, and boil, uncovered, until reduced to about ¼ cup. Reduce heat to low. Add remaining ¼ cup butter all in one piece; stir constantly until sauce is well blended, smooth, and thickened. Drizzle sauce over zucchini and fish. Makes 4 to 6 servings.

Per serving: 387 calories, 33 g protein, 11 g carbohydrates, 24 g total fat, 139 mg cholesterol, 240 mg sodium

Dinnertime is a time to relax—with flowers, candlelight,
and an elegant entrée like Sesame-crusted Sea Bass with
Zucchini (recipe on facing page). A vermouth beurre
blanc tops each serving of crisp-coated fish and squash.

Soy-basted Barbecued Catfish

Preparation time: About 15 minutes

Grilling time: 20 to 25 minutes

A rich-tasting soy-sesame baste harmonizes well with the flavors of moist, delicately sweet catfish and tender eggplant halves.

Soy Baste (recipe follows)
4 cleaned whole catfish (about 13 oz. *each*), skinned and heads removed
2 tablespoons salad oil
4 slender Oriental eggplants (3 to 4 oz. *each*)
8 green onions (including tops)

Prepare Soy Baste; set aside.

Rinse fish and pat dry. Rub surface of fish with some of the oil; then place fish, side by side, on one side of a flat hinged wire basket with handles. Close basket and secure tightly to hold fish snugly in place; set aside.

Cut off and discard eggplant stems, then cut eggplants in half lengthwise and rub all over with oil. Place eggplant halves, cut sides down, on a greased grill 4 to 6 inches above a solid bed of hot coals. Cook, turning and brushing several times with Soy Baste, until eggplants are very soft when pressed (about 10 minutes). Move to a cooler area of grill away from coals.

Place fish in basket on grill over hottest area of coals. Cook, brushing often with Soy Baste, until fish are browned on bottom. Then turn and cook until fish are just slightly translucent or wet inside; cut in thickest part to test (10 to 15 minutes *total*).

About 5 minutes before fish are done, place onions on grill over hot coals. Cook, turning once, until tinged with brown.

Remove hinged basket from grill and open carefully, pulling fish free with a fork if they stick. Using a wide spatula, transfer fish to a warm platter along with eggplants and onions. Makes 4 servings.

Soy Baste. Stir together ⅓ cup **soy sauce**, 3 tablespoons *each* **Oriental sesame oil** and minced **green onions** (including tops), 1 tablespoon *each* **vinegar** and minced **fresh ginger,** 2 teaspoons **sugar,** 2 cloves **garlic** (minced or pressed), and a pinch of **ground red pepper** (cayenne).

Per serving: 386 calories, 35 g protein, 11 g carbohydrates, 22 g total fat, 105 mg cholesterol, 1,148 mg sodium

California Orange Roughy

Preparation time: About 5 minutes

Baking time: 12 to 18 minutes

Yogurt and green onions are all that's needed to dress up New Zealand's deep-water orange roughy for a sensational quick meal. You might serve herb-buttered noodles with the fish.

1 pound orange roughy fillets
  Salt and pepper
½ cup plain lowfat yogurt
1 green onion (including top), thinly sliced
  Lemon wedges

Rinse fish, pat dry, and arrange in a single layer in a greased 9- by 13-inch baking pan. Sprinkle fish lightly with salt and pepper, then spread evenly with yogurt. Sprinkle with onion. Bake, uncovered, in a 350° oven until fish is just slightly translucent or wet inside; cut in thickest part to test (12 to 18 minutes). Offer lemon wedges to squeeze over fish to taste. Makes 3 or 4 servings.

Per serving: 162 calories, 18 g protein, 2 g carbohydrates, 8 g total fat, 24 mg cholesterol, 91 mg sodium

■ ***To Microwave:*** Rinse fish and pat dry. Lay fish in a greased 7- by 11-inch microwave-safe baking dish, overlapping fillets slightly and placing thickest portions toward outside of dish. Add salt, pepper, yogurt, and onion as directed. Microwave, covered, on **HIGH (100%)** for 3 to 5 minutes, giving dish a half-turn after 2 minutes. Let stand for 3 minutes before uncovering. Lift fish from liquid in dish to serve.

Oven-poached Monkfish

Preparation time: About 10 minutes

Cooking time: About 5 minutes

Baking time: 30 to 40 minutes

Prized for its lean, firm-textured flesh and lobster-like flavor, monkfish is also called angler and, in France, *lotte.* Poach it in white wine, then bake *en casserole* with mushrooms, Swiss cheese, and a creamy sauce. (You can poach the fish and make the sauce a day ahead, if you like.)

1½ pounds monkfish fillets
    About ½ cup dry white wine or regular-
    strength chicken broth
½ cup (¼ lb.) butter or margarine
½ pound mushrooms, sliced
⅛ teaspoon ground nutmeg
2 tablespoons all-purpose flour
   Salt
1½ cups (6 oz.) shredded Swiss cheese
   Chopped parsley

If necessary, remove silvery membrane from fish: slide a knife underneath membrane to loosen it, then pull it off from one side. Rinse fish and pat dry. Fold narrow end of fillets under to make evenly thick pieces.

Place fish in a shallow 1- to 1½-quart baking dish and add ½ cup of the wine. Cover and bake in a 400° oven until fish is just slightly translucent or wet inside; cut in thickest part to test (about 20 minutes). Remove from oven. Pour off cooking liquid from baking dish and measure it; if necessary, add more wine to make 1 cup liquid. Set aside.

Melt ¼ cup of the butter in a wide frying pan over medium-high heat; add mushrooms and nutmeg. Cook, stirring, until edges of mushrooms are brown; lift mushrooms from pan and set aside.

Melt remaining ¼ cup butter in pan; blend in flour and cook, stirring, until bubbly. Remove from heat and gradually stir in reserved cooking liquid. Return to heat and continue to cook, stirring, until sauce boils and thickens. Season to taste with salt. (At this point, you may cover and refrigerate fish, mushrooms, and sauce separately for up to a day.)

Drain off and discard any liquid that has accumulated with fish. Spoon sauce evenly over fish, then top with mushrooms and cheese.

Bake, uncovered, in a 400° oven until bubbly and heated through (12 to 15 minutes; about 20 minutes if refrigerated). Sprinkle with parsley. Makes 4 servings.

Per serving: 522 calories, 39 g protein, 7 g carbohydrates, 38 g total fat, 144 mg cholesterol, 379 mg sodium

■ *To Microwave:* Decrease butter to 6 tablespoons. Place fish and ½ cup of the wine in a 2- to 2½-quart oval microwave-safe casserole. Microwave, covered, on **HIGH (100%)** for 6 to 8 minutes or until fish tests almost done; rotate dish a half-turn after 4 minutes. Pour off and reserve liquid. In a 1-quart glass measuring cup, combine 2 tablespoons of the butter, mushrooms, and nutmeg. Cover and microwave on **HIGH (100%)** for 3 to 5 minutes or until mushrooms are limp, stirring once or twice. Lift mushrooms out and arrange over fish; set liquid aside.

Combine fish-cooking liquid and mushroom liquid; measure, then add wine, if necessary, to make 1 cup. In a 1-quart glass measuring cup, melt remaining ¼ cup butter on **HIGH (100%)** for 45 seconds to 1 minute. Using a wire whisk, blend in flour, then liquid. Cook, uncovered, on **HIGH (100%)** for 1½ to 2 minutes or until thick, stirring once or twice. Season to taste with salt.

Pour sauce over fish and mushrooms; add cheese. Microwave, uncovered, on **HIGH (100%)** for 2½ to 3 minutes or until fish is heated through, rotating dish a half-turn after 1½ minutes.

Broiled Sanddabs with Basil-Chili Butter

Preparation time: 8 to 10 minutes

Broiling time: About 4 minutes

Pacific sanddabs, a variety of sole, are favored by many connoisseurs. Here, whole or trimmed sanddabs (or thin sole fillets, if you prefer) are broiled, then topped with a spicy herb butter.

   Basil-Chili Butter (recipe follows)
4 **cleaned whole Pacific sanddabs (about ½ lb.**
   *each***), heads removed, if desired; or 1 pound**
   sole or flounder fillets (about ¼ inch thick)
   All-purpose flour
2 **tablespoons salad oil**

Prepare Basil-Chili Butter; set aside.

Rinse fish, pat dry, and dust lightly with flour. Set aside.

Place a 10- by 15-inch shallow rimmed baking pan about 4 inches below heat while you preheat broiler. Remove hot pan, pour in oil, and tilt pan to coat evenly.

Carefully turn fish in hot oil to coat. Then broil on one side only until just slightly translucent or wet inside; cut in thickest part to test (about 4 minutes).

Using a spatula, carefully lift fish from pan and slide onto plates. Dot with Basil-Chili Butter. Makes 4 servings.

Per serving: 171 calories, 22 g protein, 1 g carbohydrates, 8 g total fat, 54 mg cholesterol, 92 mg sodium

Basil-Chili Butter. In a small bowl, beat together ½ cup (¼ lb.) **butter** or margarine (at room temperature), 2 teaspoons **chili powder,** and 2 tablespoons minced **fresh basil** (or 2 teaspoons dry basil leaves). Makes about ½ cup.

Per tablespoon: 105 calories, .25 g protein, .58 g carbohydrates, 12 g total fat, 31 mg cholesterol, 124 mg sodium

Hot off the barbecue, Grilled Fish Picante (recipe on facing page) soaks up the zesty flavor of melting lime-cilantro butter. Round out the meal Southwestern style, with grill-warmed corn tortillas and crisp coleslaw accented with jicama and juicy pomegranate seeds.

Pictured on page 7

Garlic-baked Red Snapper

Preparation time: About 10 minutes

Baking time: 45 to 50 minutes

Redolent of garlic and herbs, a whole red snapper bakes to succulence in this impressive entrée for three or four friends. We suggest seasoning the fish with *herbes de Provence*, a blend containing thyme, lavender, fennel, and more; if you don't have it (or can't find it), substitute Italian herb seasoning.

¼ **cup olive oil**

2 **large heads garlic**

6 **to 8 small red thin-skinned potatoes (***each* **1½ inches in diameter)**

1 **cleaned whole red snapper or Pacific rockfish (2½ to 3 lbs.), with head and tail**

¼ **teaspoon herbes de Provence or Italian herb seasoning**

Salt and ground white pepper

All-purpose flour

1 **tablespoon butter or margarine, cut into small pieces**

Fresh herb sprigs, such as thyme, marjoram, and savory

Lemon wedges

Pour 2 tablespoons of the oil into a large, shallow baking pan (about 10 by 15 inches). Cut each garlic head in half crosswise; place halves, cut sides down, in pan. Cut potatoes into halves and arrange in pan, cut sides down. Bake, uncovered, in a 350° oven for 25 minutes.

Meanwhile, rinse fish and pat dry. Trim and discard fins just behind head. In each side of fish, make 4 diagonal slashes in a crisscross pattern (2 slashes in one direction, 2 in the opposite direction), cutting almost to the bone each time. Sprinkle with herbes de Provence; season to taste with salt and pepper. Dust lightly with flour.

Heat remaining 2 tablespoons oil in a wide frying pan over medium heat. Add fish and cook until lightly browned on both sides, turning carefully once (use 2 spatulas).

Push garlic and potatoes to edges of baking pan; set fish in center of pan. Dot with butter. Bake, uncovered, until fish is just slightly translucent or wet inside; cut in thickest part to test (20 to 25 minutes). Remove fish, potatoes, and garlic to a warm platter. Garnish with herb sprigs and lemon wedges. To serve, cut fish into chunks and lift it from the bones.

Squeeze lemon wedges and soft garlic cloves over fish and potatoes to taste. Makes 3 or 4 servings.

Per serving: 433 calories, 39 g protein, 25 g carbohydrates, 19 g total fat, 72 mg cholesterol, 151 mg sodium

Pictured on facing page

Grilled Fish Picante

Preparation time: About 10 minutes

Chilling time: At least 30 minutes

Grilling time: 10 to 12 minutes

Grilled shark steaks take on bold flavors from a salsa marinade and a topping of lime-cilantro butter.

4 **shark or salmon steaks (6 to 8 oz. *each*), about 1 inch thick**

2 **tablespoons lime juice**

½ **cup prepared mild tomato-based salsa**

Lime Butter (recipe follows)

2 **tablespoons butter or margarine, melted**

Thin lime slices

Fresh cilantro (coriander) sprigs

Rinse fish, pat dry, and place in a 9- by 13-inch baking dish. Drizzle evenly with lime juice and salsa. Cover and refrigerate for at least 30 minutes or up to 2 hours, turning once.

Meanwhile, prepare Lime Butter.

Brush fish with plain melted butter. Place on a grill 4 to 6 inches above a solid bed of medium coals. Cook, turning once, until fish is just slightly translucent or wet inside; cut in thickest part to test (10 to 12 minutes *total*).

Transfer fish to a warm platter. Spoon about 2 teaspoons of the Lime Butter onto each steak; garnish with lime slices and cilantro sprigs. Offer remaining Lime Butter to add to taste. Makes 4 servings.

Per serving: 284 calories, 36 g protein, 3 g carbohydrates, 13 g total fat, 102 mg cholesterol, 484 mg sodium

Lime Butter. Combine ⅓ cup **butter** or margarine (at room temperature), ½ teaspoon grated **lime peel**, 2 tablespoons **lime juice**, 1 tablespoon minced **fresh cilantro** (coriander), and ¼ teaspoon **crushed red pepper;** beat until fluffy. Makes about ½ cup.

Per teaspoon: 23 calories, .02 g protein, .12 g carbohydrates, 3 g total fat, 7 mg cholesterol, 26 mg sodium

Easy Oven-fried Fish & Chips

Preparation time: 10 to 15 minutes

Baking time: 25 to 30 minutes

Unlike the traditional dish, our tempting family supper of fish and chips isn't deep-fried: it bakes in the oven while you mix up your favorite coleslaw to serve alongside.

- 1 **bag (2 lbs.) frozen French fries**
- ¼ **cup butter or margarine, melted**
- ¾ **cup coarsely crushed cornflakes**
- ¼ **cup grated Parmesan cheese**
- 1 **teaspoon** *each* **garlic powder, dry marjoram leaves, and paprika**
- 2 **teaspoons parsley flakes**
- ½ **teaspoon** *each* **salt and pepper**
- 2 **pounds skinless Pacific rockfish, cod, or catfish fillets**
- 1 **egg beaten with 2 tablespoons water**
  Lemon wedges
  Malt vinegar

Spread French fries evenly in a 10- by 15-inch shallow rimmed baking pan. Bake on lowest rack of a 450° oven for 15 minutes, stirring twice. Then increase oven temperature to 500°.

Meanwhile, grease another 10- by 15-inch shallow rimmed baking pan with 1 tablespoon of the butter. Set aside. Mix cornflakes, cheese, garlic powder, marjoram, paprika, parsley flakes, salt, and pepper. Rinse fish, pat dry, and cut into strips about 2 inches wide and 5 to 6 inches long; remove any small bones.

Dip each piece of fish into egg mixture to coat; drain briefly, then turn in cornflake mixture to coat. Arrange fish pieces well apart in buttered baking pan; drizzle with remaining 3 tablespoons butter.

Bake fish on middle or upper rack of 500° oven until fish are just slightly translucent or wet inside; cut in thickest part to test (7 to 10 minutes). If necessary, leave potatoes in oven for a few more minutes to brown and crisp. Transfer fish to a warm platter, surround with potatoes, and garnish with lemon wedges. Offer vinegar to season fish to taste. Makes about 6 servings.

Per serving: 545 calories, 36 g protein, 51 g carbohydrates, 22 g total fat, 122 mg cholesterol, 635 mg sodium

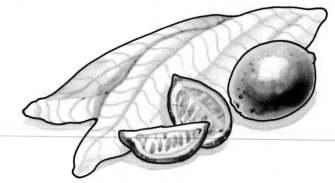

Caribbean Coconut Fish

Preparation time: 10 to 15 minutes

Baking time: 8 to 10 minutes

Coconut and lime juice give this crunchy-coated fish a flavor both tangy and subtly sweet. Depending on your tastes (and on what's available), you can make this dish with small whole trout or a variety of fish steaks or fillets.

- 4 **small cleaned whole trout (about ½ lb.** *each***); or 2 pounds white-fleshed fish fillets or steaks, such as rockfish, sea bass, or halibut (about 1 inch thick)**
- 5 **tablespoons butter or margarine, melted**
- 2 **tablespoons lime juice**
- ⅛ **teaspoon** *each* **salt and pepper**
- 1 **cup sweetened flaked coconut**
- ½ **cup fine dry bread crumbs**
- 2 **limes, cut into ¼-inch-thick slices (optional)**
- 1 **tablespoon salad oil**
- 1 **tablespoon butter or margarine**

Rinse fish and pat dry. In a shallow dish, combine the 5 tablespoons melted butter, lime juice, salt, and pepper. In another dish, combine coconut and bread crumbs.

If using whole fish, brush cavities with butter mixture. Then turn whole fish or pieces in butter mixture, then in coconut mixture to coat all sides; set aside on wax paper. If using whole fish, tuck lime slices into cavities, if desired.

Combine oil and the 1 tablespoon butter in a 10- by 15-inch shallow rimmed baking pan. Place in a 400° oven until butter is melted; tilt and swirl pan to coat with butter and oil. Place fish slightly apart in pan; sprinkle evenly with half the remaining coconut mixture. Bake for 4 minutes; turn carefully with a wide spatula, then sprinkle evenly with remaining coconut mixture. Continue to bake until just slightly translucent or wet inside; cut in thickest part to test (3 to 5 more minutes). Makes 4 servings.

Per serving: 519 calories, 30 g protein, 19 g carbohydrates, 36 g total fat, 125 mg cholesterol, 455 mg sodium

Pictured on page 74
Trout with Vegetable Stew

Preparation time: *About 15 minutes*

Cooking time: *15 to 20 minutes*

Trout from mountain stream or local market make a tempting repast when steamed atop a colorful bed of fresh vegetables.

- **2 tablespoons butter or margarine**
- **1 small onion, thinly sliced**
- **1 clove garlic, minced or pressed**
- **1 small red bell pepper, seeded and cut into ⅛-inch-wide bite-size strips**
- **1 pound zucchini or yellow crookneck squash (or ½ lb. of each), cut into ⅛-inch-thick slices**
- **1 tablespoon fresh tarragon leaves or ¼ teaspoon dry tarragon**
- **½ teaspoon freshly ground pepper**
- **3 cleaned whole trout (8 to 10 oz. *each*)**
- **Lemon wedges**
- **Fresh tarragon sprigs**
- **Salt**

Melt butter in a wide frying pan over medium heat. Add onion and garlic; cook, stirring often, until onion is limp (about 4 minutes). Add bell pepper, zucchini, tarragon leaves, and pepper; cover and cook, stirring occasionally, until squash is tender-crisp to bite (6 to 8 minutes).

Rinse fish and pat dry. Shake pan so vegetables are level, then lay fish on top. Cover and cook until fish are just slightly translucent or wet inside; cut in thickest part to test (6 to 8 minutes).

Transfer fish and vegetables to a warm platter. Garnish with lemon wedges and tarragon sprigs. Season to taste with salt. Makes 3 servings.

Per serving: 297 calories, 30 g protein, 7 g carbohydrates, 17 g total fat, 97 mg cholesterol, 153 mg sodium

■ **To Microwave:** Melt butter in an 8- to 10-inch microwave-safe rimmed plate on **HIGH (100%)** for 45 seconds to 1 minute. Stir in onion, garlic, bell pepper, zucchini, tarragon leaves, and pepper. Arrange fish, heads pointing in same direction and cavity sides down, over vegetable mixture, leaning fish against each other. Microwave, covered, on **HIGH (100%)** for 4 minutes. Give platter a half-turn. Microwave, covered, on **HIGH (100%)** for 6 to 8 more minutes or until fish are just slightly translucent or wet inside; cut in thickest part to test. Let stand, covered, for 3 minutes. Garnish and season as directed.

Breakfast Trout Fry

Preparation time: *About 10 minutes*

Cooking time: *About 35 minutes*

Pan-fried trout flank golden brown potato slices dotted with crisp bacon in this hearty weekend breakfast for campsite or patio.

- **½ cup firmly packed chopped bacon (about 3 oz.)**
- **2 medium-size thin-skinned potatoes, thinly sliced**
- **Salad oil (if needed)**
- **1 small onion, thinly sliced**
- **½ teaspoon dry thyme leaves**
- **2 cleaned whole trout (8 to 10 oz. *each*)**
- **All-purpose flour**
- **Salt and pepper**

Cook bacon in a wide frying pan over medium heat until crisp (about 5 minutes). Lift out, drain, and set aside. Spoon off and reserve 2 tablespoons of the drippings.

Add potato slices to drippings remaining in pan and cook until browned on bottom (about 10 minutes); if necessary, add oil to prevent sticking. Add onion and thyme; turn carefully with a wide spatula to mix. Continue to cook, turning occasionally, until potatoes are golden brown all over and tender when pierced (about 12 more minutes). Stir in bacon, then spoon mixture onto a warm platter and keep warm.

While potatoes are cooking, rinse fish, pat dry, and dust lightly with flour.

When potatoes are done, heat reserved 2 tablespoons bacon drippings in pan, then add fish. Cook, turning once with a wide spatula, until fish are browned on outside and just slightly translucent or wet inside; cut in thickest part to test (4 to 6 minutes *total*). Serve fish with potatoes; season to taste with salt and pepper. Makes 2 servings.

Per serving: 521 calories, 35 g protein, 36 g carbohydrates, 25 g total fat, 97 mg cholesterol, 337 mg sodium

Pot-au-Feu de Fruits de Mer

Preparation time: About 1 hour

Cooking time: 6 to 8 minutes

Baking time: About 20 minutes

A frothy tarragon sauce adds an elegant finishing touch to this oven-poached stew of seafood and julienned vegetables.

        2   tablespoons butter or margarine
      ½   cup finely chopped shallots
        3   large carrots, cut into matchstick pieces
        2   medium-size turnips, cut into matchstick pieces
        3   stalks celery, cut into matchstick pieces
        1   teaspoon minced fresh tarragon leaves or ½ teaspoon dry tarragon
        2   pounds fish fillets such as salmon, rockfish, cod, orange roughy, or lingcod (choose 1 or 2 kinds)
      12   large raw shrimp (under 30 per lb.; you need about ½ lb. *total*), shelled and deveined
      ½   pound sea scallops, rinsed and drained
      ½   cup dry white wine or vermouth
      12   mussels in shells, prepared (see page 13); or 12 small hard-shell clams in shells, suitable for steaming, scrubbed
             Bottled clam juice or Fish Stock (page 37), if needed
        3   egg yolks
        1   cup (½ lb.) butter or margarine, melted and hot
             Fresh tarragon sprigs (optional)

Melt the 2 tablespoons butter in a wide frying pan over medium heat. Add shallots, carrots, turnips, and celery. Cook, stirring often, until vegetables are almost tender to bite (6 to 8 minutes). Stir in minced tarragon. Transfer to a shallow 2-quart baking dish.

Rinse fish, pat dry, and cut across the grain into 1½- to 2-inch-wide pieces; remove any small bones. Arrange fish, shrimp, and scallops in dish with vegetables. Pour in wine. Cover tightly and bake in a 375° oven for 10 minutes.

Meanwhile, pour about 3 cups boiling water over mussels or clams and let stand just until shells open (3 to 5 minutes). Discard any unopened mussels or clams; if desired, remove and discard tops of shells from remaining mussels or clams.

After fish mixture has baked for 10 minutes, add mussels or clams. Cover and continue to bake just until fish and shellfish are done (about 10 more minutes). Fish should be just slightly translucent or

wet inside; cut in thickest part to test. Scallops and shrimp should be opaque throughout; cut to test.

Carefully pour off cooking juices; add clam juice, if needed, to make 1 cup. Keep warm. Cover seafood-vegetable mixture and keep warm.

Place egg yolks in a blender or food processor. With motor running, add the 1 cup hot melted butter—a few drops at a time at first, increasing to a slow, steady stream about ⅛6 inch wide. After you have added about half the butter, gradually add about ¼ cup of the hot cooking juices. Add remaining butter; then gradually add remaining cooking juices and whirl until blended.

Divide seafood among 6 rimmed plates or wide, shallow bowls. Surround with vegetables. Pour some of the sauce over each serving. Garnish with tarragon sprigs, if desired. Offer remaining sauce to add to taste. Makes 6 servings.

Per serving: 685 calories, 50 g protein, 13 g carbohydrates, 48 g total fat, 382 mg cholesterol, 609 mg sodium

Seafood & Mushrooms

Preparation time: About 15 minutes

Cooking time: 12 to 15 minutes

In a classic concert of flavors, scallops and shrimp cook quickly with white wine and mushrooms.

        3   tablespoons butter or margarine
        2   cups thinly sliced mushrooms
        2   cloves garlic, minced or pressed
      ½   pound sea scallops, rinsed and drained
      ½   pound medium-size raw shrimp (30 to 50 per lb.), shelled and deveined
      ¼   cup dry white wine
      ½   teaspoon paprika
        2   tablespoons chopped green onion (including top)
        1   tablespoon chopped chives (optional)
             Hot cooked rice

Melt butter in a wide frying pan over medium heat. Add mushrooms and garlic; cook, stirring occasionally, until mushrooms are lightly browned and liquid has evaporated (8 to 10 minutes).

If scallops are more than 1 inch thick, cut in half horizontally; pat dry. Add scallops, shrimp, wine, and paprika to mushrooms in pan. Stir until scallops and shrimp are opaque throughout; cut to test (about 3 minutes). Stir in onion and, if desired, chives. Serve over rice. Makes 3 or 4 servings.

Per serving: 189 calories, 20 g protein, 4 g carbohydrates, 10 g total fat, 113 mg cholesterol, 251 mg sodium

*Prize catch from the Pacific Northwest, almond-be-
decked Walla Walla Salmon (recipe on page 76) is a festive entrée. Accompany the fish with julienned zucchini.*

Sauces

&

Butters

Whether poached, grilled, broiled, or pan-fried, fresh fish may need nothing more to enhance it than a squeeze of lemon. But add a superb hot or cold sauce or a richly flavored butter, and you'll turn even the plainest fish fillet or steak into a gourmet experience.

Several toppings follow—try them all. You can make the Fennel-Pernod Butter ahead, then store it in refrigerator or freezer to slice over hot cooked fish or shellfish. Fluffy Lime Butter looks prettiest if served at room temperature. If you make it ahead, remove it from the refrigerator in advance to soften it a bit.

French-style hot butter sauces, such as Mustard-Dill Beurre Blanc and Ginger-Lemon Sauce, lend elegance to all kinds of simply cooked seafood. Pour them in a pool around fish or shellfish, or drizzle on top.

More vibrant are uncooked sauces such as Fresh Tomato-Radish Salsa, marvelous with barbecued tuna or shark steaks. Full-flavored Berry Vinaigrette adds an exciting accent to cold poached fish or shrimp presented on a bed of spinach, butter lettuce, or baby greens.

To complement steeped or grilled shrimp, pan-fried fish, or seafood-filled appetizer dumplings (such as the pot stickers on page 22), offer quick-to-make Hot & Sour Sauce. Green Apple Mignonette Sauce is a refreshing variation on a classic French sauce for oysters; it's also good with other cold cooked shellfish. Finally, dollops of Cool Dill Sauce provide a welcome finishing touch for hot or cold cooked fish such as salmon or halibut.

Fennel-Pernod Butter

⅓ cup butter or margarine, at room temperature
1½ tablespoons Pernod or anisette
1 tablespoon prepared sweet mustard
⅛ teaspoon fennel or anise seeds, coarsely crushed

Beat butter until creamy; gradually beat in Pernod until mixture is fluffy. Beat in mustard and fennel seeds.

On plastic wrap, shape butter mixture into a log 1 to 1½ inches in diameter. Wrap snugly; refrigerate or freeze until firm (at least 1 hour). If made ahead, refrigerate for up to 1 week or freeze for up to 1 month.

To serve, slice about ¼ inch thick. Place slices atop hot barbecued, broiled, or poached seafood. Makes about ½ cup.

Per tablespoon: 79 calories, .13 g protein, 2 g carbohydrates, 8 g total fat, 20 mg cholesterol, 94 mg sodium

Fluffy Lime Butter

¼ cup butter or margarine, at room temperature
1 tablespoon lime juice
½ teaspoon grated lime peel
Thin lime slices

Beat butter until creamy; gradually beat in lime juice and peel until mixture is fluffy and well blended. Spoon onto hot barbecued, broiled, or pan-fried fish; garnish each serving with a lime slice. Makes about ⅓ cup.

Per tablespoon: 82 calories, .09 g protein, .23 g carbohydrates, 9 g total fat, 25 mg cholesterol, 94 mg sodium

Mustard-Dill Beurre Blanc

2 tablespoons finely chopped shallots
⅓ cup dry white wine
1½ teaspoons tarragon wine vinegar
1 cup whipping cream
½ cup (¼ lb.) butter or margarine
1½ tablespoons chopped fresh dill or ½ teaspoon dry dill weed
1 tablespoon Dijon mustard

In a wide frying pan, combine shallots, wine, and vinegar. Bring to a boil over high heat; boil, uncovered, until reduced to about ¼ cup. Add cream, return to a boil, and boil until mixture is reduced by half (you should have about ⅔ cup).

Reduce heat to low. Add butter in one piece; stir with a whisk until butter is melted and smoothly blended into sauce. Remove from heat and stir in dill and mustard.

To keep sauce warm for up to 4 hours, pour into top of a double boiler or into a measuring cup, then set in water that is just hot to the touch. Stir sauce occasionally, replacing hot water as needed. Do not reheat or sauce will separate.

Serve with any hot cooked fish. Makes about 1 cup.

Per tablespoon: 97 calories, .41 g protein, .84 g carbohydrates, 10 g total fat, 32 mg cholesterol, 92 mg sodium

Cilantro-Lime Beurre Blanc

Follow directions for **Mustard-Dill Beurre Blanc,** but make these changes. In place of shallots, use thinly sliced **green onion** (including top); in place of tarragon wine vinegar, use 1 tablespoon **lime juice;** in place of dill, use ¼ cup lightly packed minced **fresh cilantro (coriander) leaves.**

Ginger-Lemon Sauce

½ cup *each* dry white wine and regular-strength chicken broth
2 tablespoons finely chopped shallots
1 teaspoon grated fresh ginger
¼ teaspoon grated lemon peel
½ cup whipping cream
¼ cup unsalted butter

In a wide frying pan, combine wine, broth, shallots, ginger, and lemon peel. Bring to a boil over high heat; boil, uncovered, until reduced by about half. Add cream, return to a boil, and boil until mixture is reduced to ¾ cup.

Reduce heat to low. Add butter in one piece; stir with a whisk until butter is melted and smoothly blended into sauce.

To keep sauce warm for up to 4 hours, pour into top of a double boiler or into a measuring cup, then set in water that is just hot to the touch. Stir sauce occasionally, replacing hot water as needed. Do not reheat or sauce will separate.

Serve with any hot cooked fish or with grilled skewered scallops or shrimp. Makes about 1 cup.

Per tablespoon: 50 calories, .28 g protein, .55 g carbohydrates, 5 g total fat, 16 mg cholesterol, 35 mg sodium

Fresh Tomato-Radish Salsa

1 medium-size tomato, seeded and finely chopped
¼ cup finely chopped green bell pepper
2 tablespoons *each* chopped radish and thinly sliced green onion (including top)
1 tablespoon *each* chopped fresh cilantro (coriander) and canned diced green chiles
Salt (optional)

Lightly mix tomato, bell pepper, radish, onion, cilantro, and chiles. Season to taste with salt, if desired. Serve with barbecued or broiled tuna, swordfish, or shark. Makes about 1 cup.

Per tablespoon: 2 calories, .08 g protein, .51 g carbohydrates, .01 g total fat, 0 mg cholesterol, 4 mg sodium

Berry Vinaigrette

5 tablespoons raspberry or blueberry vinegar
½ cup olive oil or salad oil
2 tablespoons minced shallots
1 teaspoon Dijon mustard
2 teaspoons honey
Freshly ground pepper

Combine vinegar, oil, shallots, mustard, and honey; mix until blended. Season to taste with pepper. If made ahead, cover and refrigerate for up to 2 weeks. Shake well before using.

Use in fish salads or drizzle over cold poached fish or cold shellfish. Makes about 1 cup.

Per tablespoon: 64 calories, .03 g protein, 1 g carbohydrates, 7 g total fat, 0 mg cholesterol, 10 mg sodium

Hot & Sour Sauce

¼ cup seasoned rice wine vinegar (or ¼ cup white wine vinegar mixed with 2 to 3 teaspoons sugar and salt to taste)
¼ cup lime juice
¼ teaspoon crushed red pepper

Stir together vinegar, lime juice, and red pepper. Use as a dip for shrimp, drizzle over pan-fried fish, or serve with pot stickers. Makes about ½ cup.

Per tablespoon: 9 calories, .01 g protein, 2 g carbohydrates, .01 g total fat, 0 mg cholesterol, 1 mg sodium

Green Apple Mignonette Sauce

1½ cups lime juice
¾ cup finely diced peeled tart green apple
3 cloves garlic, minced or pressed
3 tablespoons *each* sugar and chopped tomato
1 tablespoon anchovy paste or 3 canned anchovy fillets, minced
1½ teaspoons crushed red pepper

In a 3- to 4-cup jar, combine lime juice, apple, garlic, sugar, tomato, anchovy paste, and red pepper. If made ahead, cover and refrigerate for up to 1 month. Serve to season cold raw oysters on the half shell, or drizzle over cold cooked shrimp or crabmeat to make a salad. Makes about 2⅓ cups.

Per tablespoon: 9 calories, .12 g protein, 2 g carbohydrates, .06 g total fat, .17 mg cholesterol, 14 mg sodium

Cool Dill Sauce

⅔ cup sour cream
1 tablespoon *each* white wine vinegar and minced chives
1 tablespoon minced fresh dill or 1 teaspoon dry dill weed
⅛ teaspoon liquid hot pepper seasoning
Salt and pepper

Stir together sour cream, vinegar, chives, dill, and hot pepper seasoning; season to taste with salt and pepper. If made ahead, cover and refrigerate for up to a day. Spoon over hot or cold poached or pan-fried salmon or white-fleshed fish. Makes about ¾ cup.

Per tablespoon: 28 calories, .41 g protein, .62 g carbohydrates, 3 g total fat, 6 mg cholesterol, 8 mg sodium

*Lavish in flavor but super-simple to make, Broiled
Shrimp Wrapped in Bacon (recipe on facing page) are
carefree summer fare. Offer an almond-studded rice pilaf
and cool fresh fruit alongside.*

Pictured on page 95

Grilled Scallops in Saffron Cream

Preparation time: About 10 minutes

Cooking time: 10 minutes

Grilling time: 5 to 8 minutes

Richly gilded with a golden, creamy saffron sauce, these skewered scallops are a lovely choice for a special meal. Serve with currant-dotted rice pilaf and a bright-colored vegetable—perhaps buttered green beans or baby carrots.

- 1 **pound sea scallops, rinsed and drained**
- ½ **cup** *each* **dry white wine and regular-strength chicken broth**
- 2 **tablespoons finely chopped shallots**
  Small pinch of ground saffron (about ¹⁄₃₂ teaspoon)
- ½ **cup whipping cream**
- 1 **to 2 tablespoons butter or margarine, melted**

Pat scallops dry. On 3 or 4 thin skewers, thread scallops through their diameter so they lie flat; set aside.

In a wide frying pan, combine wine, broth, shallots, and saffron. Bring to a boil over high heat; boil, uncovered, until reduced by half. Add cream and return to a boil; if necessary, continue to boil until reduced to 1 cup. (To keep sauce warm for up to 4 hours, pour into top of a double boiler or into a measuring cup; set in water that is just hot to the touch. Stir occasionally, replacing hot water as needed. If sauce is made ahead, cover scallops and refrigerate until ready to cook.)

Brush scallops generously on both sides with butter. Place on a grill 4 to 6 inches above a solid bed of hot coals. Cook, turning once, until scallops are opaque throughout; cut to test (5 to 8 minutes *total*).

Pour sauce onto a warm platter or 3 or 4 warm dinner plates. Place scallops in sauce. Makes 3 or 4 servings.

Per serving: 221 calories, 20 g protein, 5 g carbohydrates, 13 g total fat, 78 mg cholesterol, 350 mg sodium

Pictured on facing page

Broiled Shrimp Wrapped in Bacon

Preparation time: 30 minutes

Broiling time: 6 to 10 minutes

Spectacular, yet unmatched for sheer simplicity— that's a good description of this entrée. Just wrap extra-jumbo shrimp (often called prawns) in bacon, then skewer and broil them.

- 8 **slices bacon**
- 16 **extra-jumbo raw shrimp (16 to 20 per lb.), shelled (except for tails) and deveined**

Soak 8 bamboo skewers (each 10 inches long) in water to cover for 30 minutes. Meanwhile, cook bacon in a wide frying pan over medium heat until some of the fat has cooked out and bacon begins to brown (3 to 4 minutes); bacon should not be crisp. Drain, then cut each slice in half lengthwise.

Wrap one bacon half-slice around each shrimp. Thread shrimp on soaked skewers as shown in photo on facing page.

Place skewered shrimp on a rack in a broiler pan. Broil about 4 inches below heat, turning once, until bacon is brown and prawns are opaque throughout; cut to test (6 to 10 minutes *total*). Makes 4 servings.

Per serving: 170 calories, 23 g protein, .90 g carbohydrates, 8 g total fat, 151 mg cholesterol, 338 mg sodium

■ *To Microwave:* Place bacon on several thicknesses of paper towels; cover with another paper towel. Microwave on **HIGH (100%)** for 5 minutes or until bacon is lightly browned but not crisp.

Halve bacon slices, wrap shrimp in bacon, and skewer as directed. Arrange on a microwave-safe roasting rack or several thicknesses of fresh paper towels. Cover with a paper towel. Microwave on **HIGH (100%)** for 4 to 6 minutes or until bacon is browned and shrimp are opaque throughout; reverse direction of skewers once.

Flash-in-the-Pan Shrimp & Spinach

Preparation time: About 25 minutes

Cooking time: About 6 minutes

Once you've readied all the fresh ingredients, you can whip up this main dish in a flash. Have the accompaniments at the ready before you start to cook; fluffy rice and toasted garlic bread are both good choices.

- ½ to ¾ **pound spinach, rinsed well**
- 2 **tablespoons salad oil**
- 1 **pound medium-size raw shrimp (30 to 50 per lb.), shelled and deveined**
- 3 **green onions (including tops), thinly sliced**
- ½ **cup whipping cream**
- 2 **tablespoons Dijon mustard**
- ½ **teaspoon grated orange peel**
- ⅛ **teaspoon ground nutmeg**
- 1½ **cups seedless grapes (about ½ lb.)**
  Salt (optional)

Pat spinach dry; remove stems. Set spinach aside.

Heat oil in a wide frying pan over medium-high heat. Add shrimp and onions. Cook, stirring, just until shrimp are opaque throughout; cut to test (about 2½ minutes). Lift shrimp from pan with a slotted spoon and transfer to a bowl.

To pan, add cream, mustard, orange peel, and nutmeg. Cook, stirring, until sauce forms large, shiny bubbles (1½ to 2 minutes). Return shrimp to pan along with grapes; stir gently just until heated through (about 1 minute). Remove from heat and lightly mix in spinach. Season to taste with salt, if desired, and serve immediately. Makes 3 or 4 servings.

Per serving: 310 calories, 21 g protein, 15 g carbohydrates, 19 g total fat, 173 mg cholesterol, 418 mg sodium

■ *To Microwave:* Prepare spinach as directed and set aside. Omit oil. Combine shrimp and onions in a 3- to 3½-quart microwave-safe casserole. Microwave, covered, on **HIGH (100%)** for 4 minutes, stirring once; let stand for 2 minutes. With a slotted spoon, transfer shrimp to a bowl; cover.

To casserole, add cream, mustard, orange peel, and nutmeg. Stir to blend well. Microwave, uncovered, on **HIGH (100%)** for 5 to 6 minutes or until sauce is thickened. Stir in grapes and shrimp; microwave, covered, on **HIGH (100%)** for 3 more minutes. Lightly mix in spinach, cover, and let stand for about 2 minutes before seasoning and serving.

Grilled Shrimp with Chile Paste

Preparation time: About 35 minutes

Chilling time: At least 4 hours

Grilling time: 6 to 8 minutes

Chilled yogurt sauce provides a cooling counterpoint to these boldly spicy grilled shrimp. Keep the accompaniments mild—fluffy steamed rice and a platter of sliced cucumbers and tomatoes.

- **Chile Paste (recipe follows)**
- 1 **cup plain yogurt**
- 1½ **pounds colossal raw shrimp (10 to 15 per lb.), shelled and deveined**
  Lemon wedges

Prepare Chile Paste. Mix ¼ cup of the paste with yogurt; cover and refrigerate. Mix remaining paste with shrimp; cover and refrigerate, turning occasionally, for at least 4 hours or until next day.

On each of 4 or 5 skewers, thread 4 or 5 shrimp, piercing each shrimp twice (once through head end, once through tail end). Place skewers on a greased grill 4 to 6 inches above a solid bed of hot coals. Cook, turning once, until shrimp are opaque throughout; cut to test (6 to 8 minutes *total*). Serve hot with yogurt mixture and lemon wedges. Makes 4 or 5 servings.

Chile Paste. In a blender, combine ⅓ cup **lemon juice**, ¼ cup **salad oil**, 1 large **onion** (chopped), ½ cup lightly packed **fresh cilantro (coriander) leaves**, 6 to 8 cloves **garlic**, 1 tablespoon chopped **fresh ginger**, and 1 or 2 **fresh jalapeño chiles** (seeded and coarsely chopped). Whirl until smooth.

Per serving: 264 calories, 26 g protein, 9 g carbohydrates, 14 g total fat, 171 mg cholesterol, 201 mg sodium

Squid & Bamboo Shoot Stir-Fry

Preparation time: 30 to 45 minutes

Cooking time: About 6 minutes

Thai cooks stir-fry squid with zesty seasonings, then balance the fiery flavor with plain steamed rice. Look for fish sauce in Asian markets or in the Asian foods section of a well-stocked supermarket.

1½ pounds whole squid, cleaned (see below); or ¾ pound cleaned squid mantles (tubes) and tentacles

2 tablespoons salad oil

2 cloves garlic, minced or pressed

1 tablespoon minced fresh ginger

1 small onion, thinly sliced

1 tablespoon ground California or New Mexican chiles; or 2½ teaspoons paprika plus ½ teaspoon ground red pepper (cayenne)

1 can (about 8 oz.) bamboo shoots, drained and cut into thin shreds

1 cup lightly packed fresh basil leaves

2 tablespoons white wine vinegar

½ teaspoon sugar
   About 2 tablespoons Thai fish sauce (*nam pla*) or soy sauce

Cut squid mantles crosswise into 1-inch-thick rings. On one edge of each ring, make parallel cuts about ½ inch deep and ¼ inch apart. (At this point, you may cover and refrigerate squid rings and tentacles for up to a day.)

Place a wok or wide frying pan over high heat. When pan is hot, add oil, garlic, ginger, and onion; stir-fry for 1 minute. Add ground chiles and bamboo shoots; stir-fry until bamboo shoots are hot (about 1 minute). Add squid rings and tentacles; stir-fry just until squid curls (about 2 minutes). Add basil, vinegar, sugar, and fish sauce. Stir-fry just until basil is wilted (about 1 minute). Makes 3 or 4 servings.

Per serving: 236 calories, 24 g protein, 13 g carbohydrates, 10 g total fat, 309 mg cholesterol, 64 mg sodium

How to Clean Squid

Though they're classed as shellfish, squid (calamari) don't have an external shell. Instead, there's a thin, transparent quill or cuttlebone *inside* the animal, in the mantle (the tube-shaped section).

To clean whole squid, follow these steps. First, pull on the mantle to separate it gently from the head and attached tentacles. Pull out and discard the long, clear quill inside; then, using your fingers or a spoon, scoop out and discard the material remaining in the mantle. With your fingers, pull off the thin, speckled membrane covering the mantle. Rinse the mantle well, inside and out.

Using a sharp knife, sever the head between the eyes and the tentacles; discard the eyes and attached material. Squeeze the tentacles near the cut end to pop out the hard, dark beak; discard the beak. Rinse the tentacles.

Broiled Lobster with Tomato-Basil Butter

Preparation time: About 10 minutes

Cooking time: 7 to 10 minutes

For a stylish dinner for two, serve a single 1½- to 2-pound lobster, split and broiled. For dipping, offer melted butter accented with sun-dried tomatoes and fresh basil.

1 live American lobster (1½ to 2 lbs.)

¼ cup butter or margarine

1 tablespoon finely chopped dried tomatoes packed in oil

2 teaspoons oil from tomatoes

2 tablespoons slivered fresh basil leaves

First, kill lobster. Place, stomach down, on a board and insert the tip of a sharp knife between tail section and body shell to sever spinal cord and kill lobster instantly. Then split lobster lengthwise through back shell. (If you prefer, have your seafood dealer perform these steps.)

Remove and discard stomach sac (behind head); pull out dark intestinal vein running to end of tail. Scoop out yellowish tomalley (liver) and any coral-colored roe from body cavity; if desired, mix with melted butter to make an alternate dipping sauce for lobster meat. Rinse lobster well.

Pour enough water into a large pan to cover lobster generously. Bring to a boil over high heat. Add lobster; cover. When water returns to a boil, reduce heat and simmer until meat is almost opaque in center; cut to test (3 to 5 minutes).

Meanwhile, melt butter in a small pan over low heat. Stir in tomatoes and tomato oil. Keep warm.

Place lobster halves, meat side up, in a broiler pan. Brush generously with some of the butter mixture. Broil about 4 inches below heat until meat is lightly browned on top and opaque throughout; cut to test (4 to 5 minutes). Stir basil into remaining butter mixture and serve in 2 small dishes for dipping.

To eat, twist off large whole claw where it joins body. Crack open claw and leg using a heavy cracker; pluck out meat with a small fork or metal pick. To extract tail meat, slide a fork between soft underside of tail and meat and firmly pull out meat. Dip meat in butter mixture. Makes 2 servings.

Per serving: 343 calories, 16 g protein, 3 g carbohydrates, 30 g total fat, 116 mg cholesterol, 681 mg sodium

Index

*Fresh green beans tossed with diced red and yellow bell
peppers flank tempting Grilled Scallops in Saffron Cream
(recipe on page 91). To complete a spirited menu, offer
rice pilaf dotted with dried currants and flavored with a
hint of allspice.*

95